Testimonials

I would define my relationship with God these past four years as stagnant. It was there, but not heading in any direction with any sense of passion or urgency. After reading *Alive & Free* God showed me why! I had never found my true identity in Him. I needed to change my prayers to asking God what He *wants me to know* and what He *wants me to do* in everyday situations! Now I know my identity and to function in the knowledge of who He made me to be has lifted a weight off my shoulders!

Kendra – World Traveler (Oregon)

I can't wait to follow the steps outlined in this book to discover my true identity and throw away my false identity, which until reading this book, I didn't know was false. Real thought provoker and ultimately life changing. I took notes in every chapter.

Jeff – Husband, Father & Grandfather (Oregon)

Many Christians are held back from living a life with God that is truly free. Jeff illustrates this point with life changing examples and real-life stories to reveal how you can find out who *God* says you are. If fear, anxiety, guilt and shame keep you from getting closer with God, this book contains the "key" you need to help unlock your freedom and escape the lies Satan has told you.

Aaron – Former Atheist (Washington)

Alive & Free challenges us to *discover* our true and unique God-given identity and stand firm against lies we have been told about ourselves. We are often too afraid to talk about the deepest inner struggles in our lives. The pages of this book were eye opening explaining how to be listening to the voice of the Lord more in the midst of our inner conflicts. Jeff emphasis our role to develop our discernment and how to listen to the Lord's voice.

Sam – Pastor/Teacher (India)

Alive & Free brings biblical truth from the ashes of man's convoluted conditioning that keeps us from being who we were made to be by God at the Beginning. This isn't *new thought;* this is a rebirth in hearing from God the way He intended.

Eliot – Wildlife Aficionado (Australia)

A thoughtful examination of Christian identity, and the impact of fear, guilt, and shame in our lives. Valdes explores how these forces keep us hidden in false identity, and more importantly how we can move past these barriers to discover and fully embrace our own unique nature.

Ian – Entrepreneur (Oregon)

Alive & Free

Knowing Your True Identity

J. Michael Valdes

First paperback edition (b) June 2020

www.alivefree.org
www.jeffvaldes.com

ISBN 978-1-7352111-0-7 (paperback)

ISBN 978-1-7352111-1-4 (ebook)

Cover by Calli Luikart
www.luikartink.com

Table of Contents

Foreword

I used to think that being a Christian was more about being religious than having a relationship with Jesus that was *Alive & Free.*

Jesus said, "I have come *that they may have life*, and have it to the full" and "if the Son sets you free, *you will be free* indeed."

It's easy to be influenced by the adversity of this world. We have been deceived to believe a false identity of ourselves. However, if you long for a vibrant, fresh, intimate relationship with your Creator, *Alive & Free* is for you.

I have had the privilege of calling Jeff a great friend and he has significantly encouraged me for over twenty years. Together, we have traveled the world showing people how to discover their true identity and that Jesus wants people to find their freedom in Him.

I highly recommend investing in his book as Valdes writes, "God's Word tells us that a personal relationship with Jesus is only attainable because God is the one who first seeks us out . . . God first pursues, and we must then respond to Him."

I'm excited to see the potential these truths give to all of us, as we take those needed steps closer to the One who is pursuing us. My prayer is that God will use this book to reveal to you how you can become *Alive & Free.*

Buckle your seatbelt and get ready for God to use this book and the truth from His Word to light a fire in your soul. May the Holy Spirit speak to your heart and draw you closer to Jesus as you set your life and heart on Him.

He created you, loves you, and wants you to find your true identity in Him!

Read on!

Reid Saunders
President of RSA

Preface

The end of another decade in my life drew near, and I found myself in a season of reflection. *How did I end up here?* My relationship with God had become mediocre and was not what it once was. *What had happened?*

As husband to my wife of 20 years and father to our four wonderful children, you can say my life had been blessed. My consulting business had seen its share of success, and I continued to travel around the world with a wonderful missions organization, The Berean Way, to teach forgotten people of the world how to read and study the Bible.

From the outside looking in I had it made, but deep

inside I knew the truth: my spiritual life had become rather mundane. Nothing dramatic had caused this change, but I was not where I expected I would be spiritually—at this stage of my life.

I was existing but not really *living*, I was going through the motions but not *thriving*. Bad decisions from my past lingered in the back of my mind no matter how hard I worked to keep them suppressed. I continued to raise my family in the church and build my résumé as a Christian businessman, but something authentic was missing in my life.

My passion to serve the Lord and the fire of my youth was fading, but I didn't know why. God seemed distant. When I was younger, it was natural to go first to God with my daily life issues. Over time, I found myself only reaching out to Him when things were tough and I couldn't solve those problems myself. There wasn't a specific event that caused this change, it just happened over time. Our relationship didn't feel essential, but it wasn't really broken either. To my embarrassment, God had become my backup plan.

God, I cried out one day, *come back to me! I need you*

to return to my life in a major way.

I was soon to discover that He had never left. God was waiting patiently for me because I had drifted away from Him. His answer to my prayer is where this story begins.

For years, I had turned down an invitation to hang out with a group of guys in Central Oregon for an annual weekend of fellowship and fun. This year, I finally accepted and I pleaded with God to meet me there. I wasn't even sure what that meant, but somehow, I had high expectations He would respond.

That weekend, I joined over 75 other guys who were also seeking hope, encouragement, and freedom from their own forms of bondage. Our speaker was Jamie Winship, a former law enforcement officer from Washington D.C. Decades earlier, at the invitation of the U.S. Government, he had moved his family overseas to work in high conflict areas among Muslim populations in the Middle East and Indonesia. As he told his first story, I remembered a guy who fit his description that my wife had encouraged me to pursue the previous year. (I should have listened to Erin!)

Jamie's story was amazing, but it was the truth he shared that had me transfixed. His insight into one's individual identity challenged my understanding of who I had thought I was, and his unbelievable life experiences with God seemed to have come straight from the Bible.

His core message was this: there is transformative power when we live fearlessly in our *true identity*; however, most of us are actually living in our *false identity*. The stories and truths he shared from Scripture came alive and awakened my soul.

God responded to my plea as that was exactly what I was looking for! My desire was to live in complete truth so that my actions would reflect my new perspective. He met me in a radical way that weekend and the result was a taste of *what could be. I*t rekindled a fire and woke me up to becoming more alive!

However, that reminder came quickly to the forefront of my mind that deep down I knew I still wasn't completely free. I had done many foolish things in my past, and if I were being honest, their memory continued to bring me shame and embarrassment. Although I refused to think about them, somehow they still lingered deep in the recesses of my memory like a slimy residue that would never wipe clean.

But this time I was motivated.

Was it even possible to be *completely free* from the past? *Probably not*, I thought but I wanted to believe it could be true so I pleaded with God to transform my thoughts. Obviously, I couldn't do it on my own, *but maybe He could?*

Time was what I could give, so every Saturday morning I left the house for several hours to seek, listen and talk to God. They were some of the most cherished and enlightened times of my life.

During the rest of the week, I kept having *chance encounters* where I would share my journey and all I had learned with anyone who would listen. These daily interactions with clients, friends, family and strangers confirmed these *coincidences* were consistently the perfect conversation, at the perfect place, at the perfect time, for every single one of them.

My passion grew for others to get excited about the possibility for them to discover their *own* God-given identity. Their responses were overwhelming and many people asked if I had written down all that I was learning.

Several months later, I met with Jamie for breakfast. After sharing my journey and discoveries with him, the first thing he asked was if I had journaled all that God had been teaching me. I told him I wanted to, but life kept getting in the way, and honestly, I found it a daunting task. He strongly encouraged me to take the time to record what God has been revealing to me so it could be passed on to others. I left feeling encouraged yet overwhelmed at what I knew I was supposed to do.

God continued to burden me to write about my journey. I tried to resist, but because of the persistent encouragement of some influencers in my life, here I am finally putting the remaining touches on a project I didn't think I would ever finish.

I have unabashedly expanded on Jamie's concept of identity and made it my own. The sign of a great teacher is when his work inspires others and is shared, so I hope I have done an adequate job of relaying the truths I have learned from him. The rest of this book is the result of what God has taught me through studying His Word, teaching, and disciple-making around the world over the past twenty-five years.

I'll use the terms *Christian* and *Believer* to refer to a person who agrees they have missed the mark and were full of shortcomings that they could not erase themselves. They accept that Jesus died for them, rose from the dead, and paid the penalty of their sin through the gift of grace. They have submitted to Jesus as Lord and Savior. As a result, their relationship with God was eternally restored.

Unfortunately, I believe most Christians are just like I was—disillusioned and confused why their relationship with God is more challenging and less personal than anticipated. They know what they *should believe* but they still carry baggage that they cannot seem to get rid of.

If you relate to any part of my experiences, you are not reading this book by accident.

For the person who isn't confident in what they believe, but is wanting hope, seeking freedom, and desiring truth in this broken world, this book is also for you.

Alive & Free is intended to be a practical, interactive approach that encourages you to continually ask, *how does this apply to me?* You should be empowered to understand ways where you can bring positive changes to your life and your relationship with God.

You too can be *Alive & Free* but only if you learn your true identity and are willing to become the person God created you to be.

So grab a notebook or journal to use throughout this process. Not only will we discuss the theology behind these concepts, but there are pragmatic and practical ways that can lead you to immediate and life-changing transformation with the One who created you.

I pray you will find great insights to help you dive deeper into *who God is* and discover *who He created you to be.*

Introduction

Why Are We All So Messed Up?

"In the Christian life, it's not how you start that matters. It's how you finish." —Steve Farrar [1]

"He is no fool who gives what he cannot keep, to gain what he cannot lose." —Jim Elliot [2]

Picture this: it's the beginning of a long weekend, and you've been looking forward to catching up with a close friend. The two of you sit down over cups of coffee in a quiet corner booth with nowhere to go for several hours.

What would you talk about?

Family? Work? Relationships?

Maybe your conversation drifts into sports, reality TV, politics, or even religion. Perhaps a current event gets brought up and the intensity of your conversation is fueled.

But I'm willing to guess that at some point, you'll find yourselves talking about people—perhaps people you know, or maybe those who are famous or recently in the news. The things they do or say and choices they make cause you to shake your head.

What are those people thinking? They must have some serious issues, right?

If you were able to eavesdrop on the conversations at the surrounding tables, wouldn't you discover the people around you are talking about the very same things?

Unfortunately, we have a natural tendency to pass judgment on others by using a different set of standards than we would use for ourselves. Perhaps we're not surprised that celebrities, politicians, and athletes lack perspective and seem hopelessly lost, without direction or absolute truth. But what about us?

If we turned that same focus inward, wouldn't we discover that many of those same issues, struggles, and insecurities that are so apparent in the famous also exist in our own lives (minus their large bank accounts)?

I think we would discover exactly that.

I know I did.

Our Missing Victory

But we are Christians, right? So why does that reasoning permeate our thinking as well? God promises life and freedom to those who follow Jesus, but most of us feel like we are still weighted down by sin. His promises and our reality aren't living together in unity!

So let's be honest, do you know anyone who is *truly* alive and *really* free?

I have been blessed to have met and befriend people from all over the world. I have served with them in every kind of friendship, ministry and business capacity. There are some amazing godly men, women and youth that I look up to for wisdom and advice. Yet, I can tell you honestly that almost every single one of them is not Alive & Free because they do not know their true identity.

We Christians don't often live out what we say we believe. We have our own *Christianese* language, expected behaviors, and codes of conduct, but are we living victoriously in God?

We say Jesus has set us free, yet deep down we wonder why we're not. We don't want to draw attention to our own deep flaws, so we stuff them down into secret compartments in our mind that we won't let others see.

And just like everyone else around us, we're addicted to finding ways to medicate ourselves through our daily dependence on caffeine, our over consumption of food, drugs or alcohol, and our *secret* enslavement to pornography. Messages of confusion, hypocrisy and blatant sin within church leadership have almost become normal. Recently, the news has reported that several prominent Christian public figures have renounced their faith and even taken their own lives.

Why do we see all this perplexity?

I believe it starts when we approach God with our pre-determined expectations. We want Him to react the way *we want* Him to react, but most of the time He doesn't.

Many of those problems arise when we view God through the lens of religion instead of relationship. Let me explain.

Religion vs. Relationship

Let's define *religion* as a system of rules and beliefs detailing how a person can supposedly restore their separation from a higher power, universal force, or supreme being. Religions rely on faith that their works-based rules will either gain favor and/or avoid future suffering after death. *Eternal success* is based on a person's actions.

Atheists believe their works have no impact on any kind of afterlife. They bet their eternity on the belief that nothing will happen after they die because they cease to exist. The agnostic believes the existence or nature of an afterlife simply cannot be known. Both views require a tremendous amount of faith so I refer to them as religious views as well.

In all cases, a person's religion determines their world view, which determines how they will live their life.

The Bible teaches us that real restoration with God is only possible through a *personal relationship* with Jesus. God did all the work on our behalf to bridge our separation from Him. But we must, in turn, accept what Jesus has done for us.

God's Word tells us that a personal relationship with Jesus is only attainable because God is the one who first seeks us out. But active participation from both God and a Believer are required to establish and grow the relationship. God first pursues, and we must then respond to Him. It's not so much about the *works* that we do, but rather the heart condition for *why* we do the works that we do. True Christianity is therefore better defined as a *relationship* rather than a *religion.*

Any changes in behavior out of a religious system happen because of a person's desire to self-promote and self-protect because those underlining motivations comes from our *false identities* of fear, anxiety, guilt, and shame rather than true heart transformation.

In contrast, behavioral changes from Christianity are due to the fact that God, our Creator, gives His followers a new heart, perspective, guidance, and motivation. If we combine this with our unique *true identity,* we will be well on our way to living in a special relationship with Him.

As a result, God says the only solution is for Him to provide us with a new heart. That enables internal changes within your *new* heart resulting in external behavioral changes through His love. He gives us a new understanding of what love really means. Love is a commitment to stand up for truth while bringing restoration. It is proactive, not reactive. Love does not keep score.

Understanding that as God loves us for who we are, we are able to understand how we can actually expand that love to the unlovable in our community. The more we have been forgiven, the more capacity we have to forgive those around us and desire to help restore them. Only a special kind of relationship can make this way of thinking even possible.

Based on all that God did and is doing for us, Christians should live an amazing life of freedom, right?

But as life happens, the possibility of freedom drifts further away and we're only left with more questions:

- Why do people who claim to know and love Jesus *continue to live* under the oppressive burdens of fear, anxiety, guilt, and shame?

- Why do true Christians often live lives that aren't radically different from religious, spiritual, or secular people?

- If I struggle with doubts, insecurities, and worries, does that mean I might not be saved?

- Is God punishing me for something?

- Is Jesus really alive and who He says He is?

- Can I truly understand what it means to be a follower of Christ, and how will that affect my eternity?

- I'm scared about so many situations in my Christian life, *so what am I doing wrong?*

Our Foundation

Jesus came to destroy the works of the Enemy
    —and He did.
Jesus came to make us well
    —and He did.

So why aren't we *Alive & Free*?

Do Not Be Discouraged!

It is my belief that most Christians don't understand their own unique, personal identity in Christ. In fact, they don't even realize they have one, and therefore, will not experience the freedom and quality of life they are promised. My intention is to help you discover why you were uniquely created and how to discover the name that God only calls you. It's that name that will reveal your true identity.

As we journey through this process of discovery, I ask you to keep this idea in the forefront of your mind:

> *God has given you a unique identity that is different from everyone else in the world. If you live empowered within this true identity, God will use you in unbelievable ways to change the world around you.* [3]

Let's start from the beginning of your journey into Christianity in order to understand how to become *Alive* & *Free*.

1

I'm a
Christian...Right?

"So if the Son sets you free, you will be free
indeed." —Jesus [4]

My daughter, Bella, was ten years old when she was
talking to her friend one night during a sleepover. Somehow
Jesus became the topic of their conversation. After a while,
my daughter asked her friend if she wanted Jesus to be a
part of her life. She did, and they prayed together.

The next morning, on the way home, Bella told me the
details.

"What if you messed up the prayer and didn't give her the right words to say?" I asked, wondering how she would respond.

"Dad," she responded matter-of-factly, "it's not the words you say that matter, because God knows what you mean inside your heart."

I just about drove off the road! Did that wisdom really come from my little girl?

But why would I think she is too young to understand? She has her own relationship with God who knows and loves her more than I can comprehend.

She didn't go to her friend's house with the intention of converting her. I didn't send her to do anything or tell her what to say. I hadn't thought about it. They were simply good friends talking about what is important to them. Which is how successful relationships engage with each other.

Religions, by contrast, often require their adherents to memorize, repeat scripts and report back as proof of their commitment and belief. But Bella spoke from her heart, which revealed God's true relationship with her. The story continues when later that year, my daughter's young friend helped lead both of her parents into their own relationship with Jesus. Healthy relationships are not even limited by age.

Our individual journeys with Jesus will all be

different, but some things are constant. Each of us needs to first experience a heart-changing relationship with God.

What About Your Journey?

Does any of the following sound familiar to you?

Somewhere along your adventure in life, you encounter Jesus Christ and learn He brings a different message than everyone else. All other world beliefs provide a series of rules you must keep so you can attain the afterlife, but Jesus' unique claim is that He did the work for you. Through His life, death, and resurrection, you are promised freedom that the world cannot understand and can never offer.

Deep inside your being, you believe. You commit to following Jesus. You say *the prayer*. You are what they call "born again," and your life takes off. You're no longer just one of the crowd; you are an individual part of a much bigger family. You actually talk to God as if you have direct access to the throne room of the universe—because you do.

You start attending a church regularly, join a small group, read your Bible, and pray. You meet some wonderful new people. They become your close friends and life is different. This new journey is amazing! There is a lot to learn, including the *Christianese* language, but it is an exciting time.

Everything changes. You discover God's promise to give you a new identity in Christ. You read about being a new creation, and about receiving a new heart and something about spiritual gifts. You learn that the Holy Spirit takes residence inside of you. Changes are occurring on the inside, and you actually *feel* different. Your eyes are opened, and your thinking truly changes. Some of your previous behaviors are being altered. You are a miracle, and your transformation is evident in the changes in your life.

You become vocal about your faith and start sharing your experiences with those close to you. Some are intrigued, some roll their eyes, and some are annoyed by the new you. But that's OK. You know you're on the right path, so you press on.

The Shift Begins

But over time, something happens. The relentless outside world starts to wear you down. Eventually your extreme behavior levels out a little. You might become less radical in how you follow Jesus. Maybe you tone it down a few notches. You start to come back down to reality, and your old self begins to materialize in subtle ways.

Maybe your addictions and old behaviors try to creep back into your life. Maybe your financial situation hasn't improved like you were led to believe. Maybe your health is getting worse, your spouse is still sick, your children are making bad choices, your dead-end job is going nowhere, and you are simply overwhelmed and exhausted! You feel guilty for questioning your faith, but let's face it, this Christian life is hard!

Before long, you find yourself slowly returning to some old behaviors that you thought you had escaped earlier. You start to justify this new balance in life, telling yourself that the radical changes were just a phase you went through, and that this mellower version is a more *realistic* you. Then you agree with you and you start to settle down.

One day, you find yourself staring into the mirror and wondering *where God is in all of this. He seemed so involved in the beginning.*

What happened?
Has God forgotten about me?
Did I do something wrong?
Were my skeptical friends right?
Maybe I can't be completely forgiven after all?

Perhaps you find temporary comfort during the worship service at church, or from an encouraging song on the radio, or when a friend offers you hope or wisdom. Or maybe, during a prayer of desperation, you hear the calm soft voice of the Lord reminding you He is there. But what happens when your feelings don't align with your expectations which don't align with your reality?

Slowly, you find yourself regressing backwards. You know you were changed and still feel different than you did before you trusted Christ, but it seems like the *old you* has mixed with the *new Christian you* until you basically look just like everyone else out there in your community.

You disappear back into the crowd.

You become *normal* again: living but not alive, safe but not free . . . and still crippled. And the worst part is that fear, anxiety, guilt, and shame are hovering over your soul. Doubt asks if he can come back into your life, and you welcome him in.

You don't feel free anymore.

Maybe you never were?

You thought you were a new creation, but where is the victory you were promised? Maybe what you first experienced was just temporary euphoria based on emotion? Maybe you just clung to this *religion* during a weak phase in your life?

It felt real for a while, you tell yourself, *but I just don't know anymore* . . .

It's as if you've come full circle, back to where you started.

What is Going on?

Can you relate to part or most of this story?

If being honest, the majority of Christians that I know see themselves in at least some of that journey that was just described.

Maybe you don't feel *as* discouraged, but you have settled into and accepted a life that is far less than what the Bible has promised.

Maybe your story is worse.

In my experience, most Christians have come to accept that living under oppression is the norm, though they may not realize the depth of the bondage they experience. If you stop and examine your life, you'll likely discover the weight of your bondage is heavier than you think. We have learned to suppress our anguish because we think that is what Christians do. I know I did. Without even realizing it, for nearly five decades I was teaching about freedom but living in bondage.

But now I am free.

True freedom *is* possible.

There is freedom to escape from this seemingly endless, downward cycle and you can change how your story is written. But is has to be your choice.

God is waiting for you, but you must recognize why and how you got to where you are in the first place.

2

Who Does the   **Bully Say I Am?**

"If you don't believe in the devil, try opposing
him for a while." —Unknown

"Be alert and of sober mind. Your enemy the
devil prowls around like a roaring lion looking
for someone to devour." —Peter [5]

———————————

As part of God's plan for His ultimate creation—
you and me—to love Him, He had to give us the
choice to reject Him as well. True love can't exist
without the freedom of choice. So God, in His
ultimate wisdom, created us with the capacity to both
accept and reject Him.

God can't make us love Him.

Otherwise, that would not be love.

The Bible teaches we are all born with a sin nature. Anyone who has had kids knows you don't need to teach them to be disobedient!

But sin didn't begin with Adam and Eve. The angel, Lucifer (later called Satan), was initially created without sin by God. His pride rose from within, and he chose to rebel against his Creator. He wanted to take God's place and as a result, became His enemy. [6] By definition, an enemy of God is our enemy, too. It should come as no surprise that today we are mere victims of Satan's ongoing rebellion against God.

Leonardo da Vinci's, *Mona Lisa*, might be the best-known work of art in the entire world. Imagine if this portrait decided to turn against the artist who painted her and demanded to take da Vinci's place as the Master Painter. It's ridiculous to even imagine!

So too is the idea of Satan battling against God. Think about it. There never was, nor will there ever be, any competition between the two. Satan's existence will always be finite and limited, like a painting.

It is also important to understand that God is not trying to win a war against Satan. He has already won. Rather, God's focus is in transforming our relationship with Him.

Although Satan was judged at the cross, his sentence has not yet been carried out. [7] He has been given a limited time on earth to deceive us until Jesus returns and God puts an end to all sin and restores the heavens and earth. No one knows when that will be, but during this time before He returns, God provides us the *freedom to choose* to listen to Him, or to allow ourselves to be bullied through the lies of the enemy.

The Bully's Master Plan

The Bible tells us that Satan is our ultimate oppressor. He has many names (among them are the Evil One, Enemy, Devil, Murderer, Liar, Adversary, Deceiver, and Accuser), [8] but in this book I'll refer to him simply as *The Bully.*

Bullies are terrified of who they really are, resulting in their aggressive behavior. They try to intimidate those around them through lies, force, and repetition. Bullies make a lot of noise trying to distract from their own issues, but the truth is they live in constant fear, anxiety, guilt, and shame.

The Bully lives out his identity every minute of every day. But he is limited in power, scope, and authority. He can't make us do anything, so he bullies us—God's image bearers—in the hope of pulling us away from God to fighting against each other. [9]

When Jesus' own identity was being attacked by religious leaders, He cut to the core of the Bully's identity:

"You [the corrupted religious leaders] belong to your father, the devil, and you want to carry out your father's desires. He was a murderer from the beginning, not holding to the truth, for there is no truth in him. When he lies, he speaks his native language, for he is a liar and the father of lies." [10]

He spends his time distracting us from our intended path and convinces us to stay wallowing in our previous behaviors and old identity. Even though God has forgiven us, freed us from our past, and guaranteed our future, the Bully's master plan is to keep us trapped in our ancient history.

Without even knowing it, we're constantly being groomed by him. Grooming is when someone gains another person's emotional trust with the goal of using that trust to control and exploit them. From birth the Bully uses four powerful, yet false identities to groom us: fear, anxiety, guilt, and shame.

These learned behaviors are modeled to us from the very beginning of life. In fact, a brand-new baby can be delivered *full of anxiety* prior to its first breath because of the stress passed on from its mother. [11]

Fear, anxiety, guilt, and shame make us live like we are in a fog. They're such a part of our lives that they become almost *normal*. But they are nothing

31

more than lies! If left to fester, the resulting stress can cause actual physical effects on our bodies. [12]

Deep down, we know they are keeping us in bondage, but we don't know what to do.

Let's expose these false identities to the light of God's truth.

Fear

Fear is a strong, unpleasant emotion towards someone or something that is potentially dangerous, painful, or threatening. It paralyzes us, and because our minds are occupied by potential harm, we are unable to live freely in faith.

What we forget is this: fear can do nothing without our complete cooperation. The Bully keeps telling us how things can go wrong, but his lies are only as effective as our willingness to listen and believe them. And for some foolish reason, we keep allowing the Bully to tell us why we need to be more afraid. If you think about it, living in fear takes far more effort and energy than living in faith.

But what does the Bible say about fear?

> Fear not, for I have redeemed you; I have called you by name, you are Mine. [13]

> For God has not given us a spirit of fearfulness, but one of power, love, and sound judgment. [14]

In fact, Jesus goes out of his way to tell us that while the world brings fear, He offers us peace. He tells us, But seek first the kingdom of God and His righteousness, and all these things will be added to you. [15]

For clarification: *fear*, in the right sense, is an important component of the Christian life. We're told, "The fear of the Lord is the beginning of knowledge" [16] and the Bible talks frequently about fearing God, meaning respect, awe, and submission. Remember, the English language can be confusing as there are often multiple meanings for the same word depending on its context. For example, the word *bear* can mean 1) to carry, 2) to hold up or support, 3) to put up with, endure, 4) to strongly dislike, or 5) a hairy carnivore mammal. Throughout this book, I'm using "fear" to refer to those negative feelings or distressing emotion rather than a measure of respect.

Anxiety

Anxiety or worry happens when you take on a responsibility for the future that God never intended for you to carry. It is the bottling-up of emotions. Anxiety is the anticipation that horrible events can come crashing down on you at any time that you can't control. It quickly derails you from the freedom God has called you to live.

My grandfather constantly told us, "I worry about you because I love you." Wait, what? Worrying equals love? I don't think so.

Worrying about circumstances you don't have control over is exhausting. It will keep you from engaging in the important tasks. Life brings very real challenges every day, and if we start our morning with anxiety, we're already defeated.

Anxiety is best combated through active communication with our Creator. He replaces our worry with love, which is expressed through service, self-sacrifice, patience, and kindness.

What does the Bible say about anxiety?

> Anxiety in a man's heart weighs him down, but a good word makes him glad. [17]

> Do not be anxious about anything, but in everything by prayer and supplication with thanksgiving let your requests be made known to God. And the peace of God, which surpasses all understanding, will guard your hearts and your minds in Christ Jesus. [18]

Guilt

If anxiety is the Bully's attempt to get us negatively focused on the future, then guilt is His attempt to keep us living in the past and unable to move forward. Guilt nullifies God's promise of forgiveness—if we allow it to. It bogs us down, and we are rendered actionless, which is the opposite of the life of freedom God has given us. The Bully will even try to get us to feel guilty about things we *didn't* do. We were never meant to dwell on guilt, so even a short amount of time spent here is paralyzing.

What does the Bible say about guilt?

> Then I acknowledged my sin to you and did
> not cover up my iniquity. I said, "I will
> confess my transgressions to the Lord. And
> you forgave the guilt of my sin." [19]

> Therefore, there is now no condemnation for
> those who are in Christ Jesus, because through
> Christ Jesus the law of the Spirit who gives life
> has set you free from the law of sin and death. [20]

Shame

Shame is a sense of inadequacy, dishonor, or regret that results from listening to guilt. It tells us we are unworthy of the love God freely offers us and that *we need to hide from Him.* We experience shame when we choose to listen to the voice of the Bully instead of the voice of our Savior. The Bully uses shame to take us out of the game of life, and when we give in to it, we willingly surrender to his control.

What does the Bible say about shame?

> So, if the Son sets you free [and He has], you

will be free indeed. [21]

Anyone who believes in him will never be put to shame. [22]

Knowing Is Half the Battle

Why does the Bully spend so much time and energy grooming us to live in fear, anxiety, guilt, and shame? So he can take us out of the battle for God and render us unable to help and serve others.

My friend Jamie Winship says, "The enemy always attacks your identity first, because once you lose your identity, you have no idea what to do next."

Could it be that the false identities he pushes on us help prove his existence? Perhaps this is best explained by a quote I once heard from an old woman in the former Soviet Union: "We always knew there was a God—otherwise they wouldn't keep telling us He didn't exist!"

The false identities of fear, anxiety, guilt, and shame are like a cancer growing in the unseen places of our hearts. They can be removed, but if left to fester and grow, they will eventually kill us.

Years ago, when I was having lunch with my mom, she noticed an abnormal mole on my arm so I had it immediately removed. The lab tests came back a few days later – this cancer was malignant! The doctor explained this type of skin cancer was the most curable and also the deadliest. If identified early enough, the entire disease could be removed. If not, it would grow deep enough until it entered the bloodstream. At that point, nothing more could be done.

Thankfully, the malignancy was removed in time, and I have been cancer-free for ten years. In the same way, God can heal us and set us from these false identities, once we are aware and work to have them removed permanently from our lives.

Jesus offers, but doesn't guarantee us freedom. That means the Bully has to keep persuading us to give him control over our lives. Ironically, *we* have to help him or his grooming will be ineffective! He does not have the power or authority to make these changes in our lives without our cooperation. All he can do is to remind us of his lies and bully us into choosing to believe them.

> For clarification: The Bible says we all battle three enemies: Satan, our *flesh*, and the *world*. [23] Although different, all three work in similar ways. Throughout this book I am going to focus mainly on the Bully, but you can also replace him with the terms flesh or the world as well.

The Bully's strategy couldn't be clearer. He can't control you unless you agree to believe in the false identities of fear, anxiety, guilt, and shame. Unless you hand over the controls to the Bully, he has no control over you. But he is very good at manipulation and freedom is easier said than done.

The simple truth is, you don't have to surrender that control to the Bully anymore.

So where do we go from here?

3

Prison Is Not   Your Home!

"I am the Lord; I have called you in righteousness;
I will take you by the hand and keep you . . . to
bring out the prisoners from the dungeon, from
the prison [literally "bondage of sin"] those who
sit in darkness." —God [24]

Imagine this. You're born a prisoner, confined to an old, dark, filthy jail. It's where you call home and spend your entire life. There is no hope of ever leaving this place.

However, once you commit to follow Jesus,

something incredible happened: He handed you the key to release that lock that had kept you trapped. You were instantly emancipated from your bondage!

Immediately discharged, Jesus invites you to follow Him away from the prison grounds into a new world of freedom. *Just leave the key in the lock behind you because you will never use it again. Walk away and don't look back and I will show you how to become Alive & Free!*

But on your way out the Bully screams from behind and you stop. He reminds you of your false identities. Doubt creeps in and you question the unknown journey ahead of you.

Where will I go?

You look around. You get scared and panic. Instead of continuing forward to follow Jesus to freedom, you just freeze. Confused, you turn and look behind you back into your old, dark cell. There is nothing compelling to draw you back but it is familiar and known. The Bully keeps yelling at you. Dejected, you reverse your course and return.

You enter, shut the door behind you and remove the key from the lock. You hold on to it tightly. As you sit back down and look through the jail cell out into a world of potential freedom, deep down you know where you truly belong. Your false identities are powerful and they are not going to allow you to leave.

You justify, *I still have the key so I can come and go as I please, right? Isn't this key my endorsement to freedom?* As you stare at your hand, *don't I finally have the control I seek?*

You can justify all you want, you ventured out a little farther but you ended up in the same place. This isn't life nor freedom.

Toss That Key and Walk Away

The reality is we are all born into captivity and bondage due to our sin nature. [25] But when Jesus took our sins upon Himself, He received the full consequences that were supposed to be for us and our debt was completely vindicated. Why then do we Christians refuse to leave our old prison cell? No matter how great the freedom that Jesus offers, we somehow find ourselves preferring to stay in the familiarity of our former captivity. Why are we afraid of going into the unknown with God when He dramatically proved His love by offering us the ultimate sacrifice?

We have been bullied for so long that we find it hard to believe we can truly be *Alive & Free* like God promises. We tell ourselves freedom is possessing the key to unlock at will the door to our old prison cell. But that *key* isn't freedom. Freedom is freedom. In reality, true freedom is throwing away the key and leaving the prison yard far behind, never to return.

Unimaginable adventures lie ahead of us. We were meant to explore a world full of possibilities with Jesus as our guide, but we have to be willing to stand up and walk towards freedom. You have to follow Him *by leaving* your former prison cell forever!

If you're like me, you want to live with purpose and serve God faithfully. You don't want to stay stuck in your former ways! But when Christians are constantly told to *do more* (like pray more, read more, serve more, love more, etc.) that won't lead to freedom or alter our behavior. An intimate relationship with our Creator does, and only this will motivate us to seek Him on deeper levels.

Zig Ziglar said, "If you aim at nothing, you will hit it every time." That seems to be the unintentional life plan for many Christians that I know. Not because they don't want to grow, but because they just don't know what to do. And then we keep telling each other to *just be better*.

But we are not better! We *have been* truly transformed, so why do most Christians live like they are dead, rather than *Alive & Free*? Why, if we were able to peek behind the curtain of their lives, would we see that a majority of Believers still live in the false identities of fear, anxiety, guilt, and shame? I believe it's because we don't really know who God says we are, and therefore, we don't live like He wants us to live. What's missing is that we are lacking knowledge of our true identities.

If your doctor prescribes lifestyle changes in order to restore your health, but you decide to only implement a few of her recommendations, you won't get the results you seek. Likewise, I believe Christians, in general, have practiced the same thing *spiritually* by only accepting part of God's truth about our identity, and therefore, we can't see who we really are. We shouldn't be surprised, then, that we find ourselves still unhealthy and still willingly stuck in our former prison cells.

A Sinner No More

Let's start with our language. What we say often indicates what we believe. Consider the following Christian sayings, which demonstrate a lack of understanding about our relationship of God and our need to embrace our true identity from Him:

God helps those who help themselves.

If we stop and think about this, doesn't this phrase sum up why humanity is in this mess in the first place? As Adam and Eve discovered, self-reliance is a sure way to get ourselves into deeper trouble. We desperately need God, because we don't have the resources within ourselves to break free and live victoriously. This statement is not Scriptural.

Instead, Jesus said, If anyone wishes to come after Me, he must deny himself, and take up his cross and follow Me. [26]

Maybe a better phrase is "God helps those who don't deserve it."

God won't give you more than you can handle.

Who are we kidding? Life gives us more than we can handle every single day! That's why we have addictions, pornography, chronic health, and the entitlement mindset in our culture. It's also why we need to replace those with a daily, intimate relationship with God. We face obstacles daily that try to take away our hope and our joy. God doesn't promise to take away our problems, but He will never leave us through even our most difficult circumstances.

Come to Me, all of you who are weary and burdened, and I will give you rest. [27]

Maybe a better phrase is "When you get more that you can handle, God is waiting to lift you up."

The Devil made me do it.

Really? The Bully can't make you do anything! All he can do is offer you suggestions and tempt or threaten you with the hopes that you listen to his voice and hand more control of your life over to him. [28]

He needs you to buy into his lies and false tactics.

47

He desperately wants you to feel helpless, powerless, and without hope. Then you quit being who God made you to be. The Bully wants to control you like a circus elephant that picks up the tiny stake it is tied to and moves it where its handler tells him to go. Both the stake and the small rope it is attached to could be broken with minimal effort, but from an early age, the elephant has been trained to submit to them.

Maybe a better phrase is "The Devil can't make me do *anything*."

I'm just a sinner saved by grace

Don't get me started on this one. This phrase might be the Bully's greatest deception among Christians.

Let's unpack this. *Sinner* was your identity at birth. But at the very moment Jesus became your Lord and Savior, *sinner* became your old identity. However, the Bully has duped the Body of Christ into holding on to this belief.

If you refer to yourself as a sinner, after you've decided to follow Jesus, then you are actually denying God's truth. You are rejecting the Good News of the cross and what Jesus did for you.

Besides being bad theology, this widely accepted statement keeps us trapped in our prison cell and halts our growth and maturity. Worse yet, the mindset it represents provides Christians with an excuse to continue to live a life that is not free from sin.

As part of your transformation, Scripture teaches that God gave you a new heart and new spirit. [29] Jesus says you are *born again*. [30] The apostle Paul says you are a *new creation* and *the old [you] is passed, and the new [you] is come*. [31] Even though you have the freedom to choose to act in sinful ways, identifying as a sinner is a false identity for you.

You may ask, "But I still make bad choices, so doesn't that make me a sinner?"

No, it does not. As you live life here on this earth in your fleshly body you will still sin as Scripture says, not a single person on earth is always good and never sins. [32] But that does not make you a sinner! We need to stop believing this lie.

Understanding and believing that a follower of Jesus *can no longer* identify as a sinner seems to be one of the most challenging truths for us to comprehend. Committing a sin will not change the true identity God has given you. It just means you made a bad choice.

The process is simple. When you sin, repent and ask for forgiveness immediately. Otherwise, you will be giving the Bully the opportunity to try and convince you to return to your old false identity, that of sinner.

You did nothing to earn your true identity from God, and therefore, you can do nothing to change it or lose it. However, you can choose to believe the lies of the Bully over the truth from God. You *do* have control over that.

A better phrase is "I am not a sinner. I am *Alive & Free* and saved by grace!" Now shout that out loud!

Sayings like these have kept Christians in bondage for thousands of years because they allow us to justify not being *Alive & Free.* When we accept less than what God has for us, it becomes easier for us to excuse living in bondage and remaining in our old cell.

Christians and Lust

Let me give an example of how embracing our false identity keeps us imprisoned. I have participated and led multiple men's groups during my lifetime, and the issue of lust is probably the most common struggle for us. A woman walks by, and we visually look her over. Our excuse? *"What can I do? God made us visual creatures."* We justify that we can't help but stare because it is not our fault. In fact, it's natural for us to view women like this.

Christians (both men and women) *apparently* lack strength to fight lust because *"God made us this way."* So somewhere along the line, probably with good intentions, someone came up with a set of *Christian* rules. As we justify our behavior, we give the Bully authority to deceive us.

See if you can follow along with this supposedly *Christian* logic.

We needed to come up with a way to rationalize our actions, so we determined there is a difference between looking (a quick glance) and lingering (staring) at someone else. It goes something like this:

"We can look, because God made beauty for us to enjoy. But don't you dare let your gaze linger, because that will lead to lust (sin)!"

So how do we define lingering? *"If we hold a stare for, let's say under 2.5 seconds, will we be safe? Can we agree to that? Good."* The unofficial rule is now established that as long as you don't stare at someone for any longer than 2.5 seconds you will be in the Christian safe-zone.

And here we go again. We just turned a heart issue into another Christian formula, enabling us to embrace a false identity instead of living in our true identity.

So let's return to our accountability group. After the typical small talk, the conversation turns personal, and it goes down something like this:

The peer or mentor says, "I've got to ask. Did you lust, view pornography, hold a lingering glance over 2.5 seconds, or flirt with a co-worker this week?"

In response, one man tells a blatant lie: "No, I did not!"

The mentor responds: "That's great! I told you God can set you free. The enemy will keep attacking you, but we are in this together. Let's celebrate the victory that comes in Jesus! Isn't it great to be free and to know you don't have to live that way anymore? Let's make it two weeks in a row. I'll keep praying for you."

The man thinks to himself, *I'm terrible! I'm a failure!* Fear, anxiety, guilt, and shame grip him even tighter, and he is more hopeless than ever.

Another man says in response to the same question, "No, not really." He justifies this to himself, thinking, *it's not porn per se, it was in one of those grey areas. However, it was an improvement over what I was doing last week, so yes, actually I am doing better. Right?*

Maybe he didn't break any of the technical sins, but if he were being honest, there was still some form of lusting in his heart.

Again, the mentor responds eagerly. "That's great!"

This man also thinks to himself, *I'm terrible! I'm a failure!* He too experiences fear, anxiety, guilt, and shame, resulting in hopelessness.

Or consider this last potential response. When asked, another man responds, "Yes, I blew it! Again!"

The mentor says: "Come on, man! What are you thinking? You know I'll be here to love you, but you have got to think about your wife and your kids. You're free from all this and you don't need to go there. Why do you want to live in such guilt? Keep fighting. Keep praying. Keep reading your Bible. God is going to set you free from this bondage. I'll check in next week but call me if you start to struggle. Maybe we should get a software program for you to install on your computer to alert me when you fail. You can do this, man!"

You can probably guess this man's response. He too thinks, *I'm terrible! I'm a failure!* Fear, anxiety, guilt, and shame overwhelm him, leaving him hopelessly trapped.

This may seem like a negative attitude toward Christian accountability, but I believe there is real truth here. We need to stop deceiving each other and learn to deal with the core issue—*we don't know our true identity.* Remember, God doesn't want us to just live *mostly* free.

Please don't get me wrong: accountability *is* necessary for everyone. I've seen deliverance and heard encouraging stories of victory that came out of accountability groups. I personally know people who were set free overnight from life-long addictions. But if your experience is anything like mine, you easily fall back into the same routine feeling more fear, more anxiety, more guilt, and more shame. Eventually, many men and women stop attending these groups because they don't see any long-term victory in their lives. They're still trapped.

This cycle repeats itself with Christians over and over again, year after year. And it's not only the issue of lust. We have applied the same Christian logic to white lies, *borrowing* from others, overeating, alcohol, gossip, swearing, and just about every other sin. It has been very discouraging as a Christian leader to see the lack of long-term success in Believers' lives, whether it comes to overcoming addiction, pornography, gluttony, anger, lust, lying, or cheating.

If God's promises are true, why aren't we seeing more people living like they are really alive? Don't the promises of Scripture and the heart of our Creator demand that we should witness an explosion of freedom when we follow Jesus?

But as we've observed, Christians are not living in their true identity, even though they have been set free from the bondage they were in prior to meeting Jesus. That means we're still in our prison cell.

Instead of pursuing our relationship with God, we're looking for the perfect formula to get our desired results. But God doesn't work in formulas. Every situation is unique, and each individual has a personal relationship with Him.

The Bully wants us to focus on who we were (a sinner separated from God) and helps us develop a set of rules to make us stay in that false mindset and remain imprisoned. We're still listening to the voice of the wrong advisor.

So we return to that old cell, along with a lot of other Christians just like us. And discouragement isn't far behind. I know because I kept returning to my imprisonment, too. The more years I lived, the more frustrated I got when I found myself in this seemingly endless and defeated position.

Do we just give in? No way!

Is there really a way out? You bet.

God isn't surprised, discouraged or angry. He wants you to escape for good!

You Are Not Alone

Remember that God knows it is challenging to follow Him in complete obedience while living here on earth. Relationships are messy. Perfection cannot be attained in this life, but He expects growth and correction as He exposes our selfishness.

- Ancient proverbs remind us, A dog returns to its vomit, **and,** A sow that is washed returns to her wallowing in the mud. [33]
- Paul the Apostle is surprising in his honest personal assessment: My problem is that I am of the fallen human realm . . . I am not able to do the things I want; and at the same time, I do the things I despise. [34]
- The Apostle Peter was once rebuked by Paul for displaying hypocrisy in public. [35]

The Bully wants us to believe that any kind of

failure brings God's immediate disappointment and wrath upon us. But this is not true! God knows the process we all go through will include times of failure and rebellion. Thankfully, His love is not contingent on our actions. He walks alongside us, helping us grow and mature in Him. Of course, He does not approve of our poor choices, but they will never change His view of us.

Ready to Break Free?

God not only wants us out of our former cell—He desires to completely remove us away from the prison ground. Freedom is not holding onto that key. Freedom is not an unlocked jail cell.

Freedom is abandoning that prison compound completely. *But it is up to you!* You have to choose to leave and then act on it. Jesus waits for you to follow Him away from your past and towards a more fulfilling life.

God won't drag you out of that cell against your will, but He will keep encouraging you to join Him so He can take you far away from those former chains of bondage.

If you start to develop your relationship with God and learn who He made you to be, you would be too busy to get derailed by your old, false identities and would have no time nor interest in returning to the prison cell.

The freedom that comes from being released is overwhelming, but it pales in comparison to what God has in store for you because you were created for so much more than what you think you know.

If you're ready, it's time for a jailbreak!

4

One Coin, Two Sides

"If any of you lacks wisdom, let him ask God,
who gives generously to all without reproach,
and it will be given him." —James [36]

While attending seminary, I was drawn to the theology of a new Christian's identity rather than the practical advice on how to live it out. As I grew wiser through my travels around the world, my priority shifted towards teaching on the practicality of one's identity.

In his book *Birthright*, which has greatly impacted me, David Needham shared how our actual identity is changed by God as soon as we chose to follow Jesus:

> God tells us we are alive in a way we have never been alive before, possessing a birthright we never possessed before. In that moment when we received Christ, God's miraculous "birthing" act gave us value, a beauty, a preciousness that lifts us above all earthly measurements. He encourages us to look deep within his workmanship and make that unexpected discovery of passion for him and a holiness that will set us free to be ourselves—free to live and to love. [37]

This made so much sense to me! Since God pursued a relationship with me when I was His enemy, it was logical that He would also make changes within my heart to help me learn who I was called to become.

I thought I understood my general identity in Christ as part of His body, but my unanswered question was, *what is my specific role in all of this?* I wanted to live within *His* purpose.

Deep down, I believed there was more to a person's *identity* than what I had understood. I wouldn't say I had an incomplete understanding, I just felt like there was a deeper level I hadn't yet discovered.

The Other Side of the Coin

Decades after seminary, God sent me to Central Oregon to meet Jamie Winship—who I introduced in the Preface—to hear him discuss his insights. I considered identity to be *my* subject, and I couldn't wait to hear what God might teach me through Jamie. I believed He would meet me there in a life-changing way.

Jamie started out by sharing ideas I was familiar with, but then he took an unexpected turn. Using the Scriptures and almost unbelievable personal experiences, he explained that at birth, each of us is given a unique identity by God. We all know God made us physically unique, as even identical twins have physical differences. But He also gave each of us a true *spiritual* identity that no one else in the world has been given.

Our true identity cannot be changed or

modified because it was given by our Creator. And if we live within that identity, He will use us to change the world.

How differently would you approach your life if you knew what your unique identity was? My mind took off and I wondered, *did I have a unique identity?*

Jamie shared truths that fit perfectly within my life experiences, but I had never heard identity explained this way before. It wasn't quite familiar, but it wasn't exactly new to me, either. One thing was certain, this message resonated with my soul.

I wanted more!

After Jamie finished sharing, I sat by myself out on this large outdoor deck under the giant pine trees of Central Oregon, enjoying the beautiful spring afternoon. I reached my hand into my pocket and pulled out a quarter. As I stared at it, I heard God tell me to flip it over.

"What is this?" I asked.

The other side of the coin, I sensed Him say.

And I knew exactly what He meant.

This was the missing piece I had been seeking. I had only been teaching part of the truth about our identity. It wasn't wrong, but it wasn't complete.

Right then and there, God completed the concept of identity for me. The first side of the coin represented my identity as a part of the collective body of Christ. It is all of us Christians together.

The flip side represented *my own unique identity*. It was the particularness that God had given only to me. My understanding of identity had been made complete! This was the solution to a mystery I had spent years of my life trying to solve.

In the movie *Raiders of the Lost Ark*, a medallion detailing the resting place of the lost Ark of the Covenant was needed to identify its location. At one point, the Nazi Gestapo agent Toht grabbed the burning hot pendant, unaware it had been heated in a fire. Toht escaped without the medallion, but the image from one side was seared into his palm. Later in the movie, we learn the Nazis were digging for the Ark in the wrong location. They didn't understand that the other side of the medallion completed the instructions to locate the Ark's resting place. They were so close, but the absence of both sides of the pendant had them missing out on the treasure because they lacked the whole truth.

Likewise, most Christians struggle because they do not know who they are as individuals. Being a part of the Body of Christ is fairly easy to comprehend. However, we're lacking "the other side of the medallion," which is the unique and special name God calls each of us individually. As a result, we are unable to realize our true identity.

The Coach's Personal Message

Picture an entire sports team gathered in the locker room where the head coach gives a speech during a break in the game. Everyone is there: the defensive, offensive, special teams, substitute players, the coaches, assistants, and managers. No matter their role, they all hear the same message and are dismissed to finish the game.

This is how I picture the Christian life is for most people. We are passionate and trying our best to win, but sincerity alone doesn't bring victory. Many are satisfied to have made the team and have the right to wear the jersey.

However, what if on your way out of the locker room, you notice Coach standing off to the side, motioning to you. Instead of running back out on the field with the rest of the team, you head in a different direction.

Coach pulls you aside for a personal teaching moment where you are given unique instruction and encouragement on how you are to proceed based on *your* specific role on the team. You are told how valuable your job is, and that the team's success is dependent on you doing what you have been recruited to do. Then Coach tells you that only you can do this task.

A fire stirs inside you, and you confidently accept the challenge. Only then are you sent out to join the rest of your team. Now you have purpose and understand the greater role you have been given for your entire team to be successful.

Likewise, God has been waiting to pull you aside

every day to provide that personal instruction. However, most of us just run back out onto the field and don't even pay attention to Him because we aren't looking for Him. But He's right there motioning and waiting for each of us to stop, turn towards Him, and receive our unique instructions.

He doesn't demand attention like the Bully so it's been easy for us to just run on by without even noticing what we are missing. After all, we think we won once we made the team (when we were saved). So what more do we have to live for except to wait around until we die and go to heaven? That sounds cynical, but if we are honest, I think it is true for far too many of us.

Frankly, because many of us Christians don't *really know* God, we aren't actually looking for or listening to Him. However, the truth is you are hearing someone's message. We all are.

In real life, those that make the most noise receive the most attention, and that includes our peers, social media influencers, musicians, celebrities, and even family. Is it any wonder why Christians are struggling to find their true identity when their main influences come from those who do not know Jesus?

The moment of our salvation was only the beginning of our walk with God, but we often view that event as the pinnacle of the Christian existence. As awesome of a miracle as it was to become a follower of Jesus, that was *only the beginning*. Jesus saved you so that you could get to know God and His calling for your life. As we move forward from there, our personal relationship with Christ should blossom and grow, not become stagnant and die. But most of us haven't taken the time needed to develop that relationship and hear His personal instructions.

That is why we are not *Alive & Free*.

So God waits for you to approach Him.

Patiently.

He has something very important to say to you and you alone about your specific identity.

So what is the name He calls you?

5

What's in a Name?

"Therefore the Lord himself will give you a sign: The
virgin will conceive and give birth to a son [Jesus],
and will call him Immanuel [literally *God with us*.]"
—Isaiah [38]

The concept of *naming* in the Bible appears to carry
much more significance than just labeling something for
convenience or pleasure. It seems to provide us readers of
the story with an insight into the narrative as to what lies
ahead. Recognizing the uniqueness associated with a *name*
is critical to understanding the rest of this book. There are
many different examples in Scripture.

Territories were often named to celebrate or remember

events.

- So Abraham called that place The Lord Will Provide [lit. *to see or perceive, to be shown or to understand*]. [39]
- David said, "As waters break out, God has broken out against my enemies by my hand." So that place was called Baal Perazim [lit. *place of breeches*]. [40]
- Then the LORD said to Joshua, "Today I have rolled away the reproach of Egypt from you." So the place has been called Gilgal [lit. *a wheel or rolling away*] to this day. [41]

We also see this with wells, [42] altars, [43] pillars, [44] and fields. [45] Even physical characteristics [46] and animals [47] influenced what parents would call their children.

Throughout history, the process of naming people was often "rooted in the ancient world's understanding that a name expressed essence. To know the name of a person was to know that person's total character and nature. Revealing character and destiny, personal names might express hopes for the child's future." [48]

God further displayed this significance when He intervened on rare occasions to clarify one's true identity by re-naming them.

- Abram [lit. *exalted father*] became Abraham [lit. *I am making you the father of many nations.*] [49]
- Sarai [lit. *my princess*] became Sarah [lit. *mother of nations*] declaring God's impossible promise to her.

- Jacob [lit. *supplanter or deceiver*] became Israel [lit. *because you have struggled with God and with men, and you have won.*] [50]
- Jesus changed Simon [lit. *listening or hearing*] to Peter or Cephas [lit. *rock.*] [51]

This practice of re-naming later occurred in other cultures as well:

- After being removed from Israel, in an attempt to dissolve their remembrances of God, the Babylonian King renamed Daniel [lit. *God is my judge*], Hananiah [lit. *God has been gracious*], Mishael [lit. *who is what God is*] and Azariah [lit. *God has helped*]. They were re-identified after local Babylonian gods to Belteshazzar [lit. *Bel will protect*], Shadrach [lit. *inspired of Aku*], Meshach [lit. *belonging to Aku*], Abednego [lit. *servant of Nego*] in an attempt to alter their identity. [52]
- Naomi [lit. *beautiful*] when suffering through the loss of her family pleaded with her people to now call her Mara [lit. *bitter*]. [53]
- John the Baptist was intentionally not named *Little Zechariah* at birth as expected, allowing him to follow a different life path than that of his father. [54]
- Scripture even hints that names can be changed through a message, blessing or a future promise. Blessed are the . . . (*peacemakers*, etc.) for they will be called . . . (*children of God, etc.*) [55]

- Most marriages today still involve the changing or modification of the last name of one or both of the spouses.
- It is not uncommon for people to change their birth names due to a variety of circumstances like adoption, divorce, nationality association, etc.
- African first names are often influenced by factors like events surrounding the baby's birth, emotional warnings or moods of the family during the birth, celebrity culture, order of birth, faith and religion, time of day and day of birth, ancestry, and more. [56]
- Native American tribes, such as the Sioux, had a complicated naming system with six classes of names which incorporated Birth Names, Nicknames, Honor Names, special deed Names, Secret and Spirit names. [57]
- Friends refer to each other by nicknames identifying them back to events that were often heroic, embarrassing or downright silly. I have at least 10 nicknames given to me from my college years alone!

Name Does Not Guarantee Responsibility

Remember, there is no assurance that your name will reflect your actions, as intent does not guarantee an outcome. *You still have to make the right choices.*

To the angel of the church in Sardis write: He who

has the seven Spirits of God and the seven stars, says this: 'I know your deeds, that you have a name that you are alive [lit. among the living], but you are dead [lit *a corpse*]. [58]

The Berean Way

Now that my understanding of identity included the *other side of the coin*, I needed confirmation of this truth in the Scriptures. So, to the Bible I went.

I've been inspired by a particular group of people from the town of Berea, located in northern Greece, who were mentioned briefly in the Book of Acts:

Now the Berean Jews were of more noble character than those in Thessalonica, for they received the message with great eagerness and examined the Scriptures every day to see if what Paul said was true. [59]

It was not uncommon for teachers to travel throughout the then civilized world and share their ideas. The Bereans seemed to be open to learning new teachings; however, they held the truth in the highest esteem and examined the Scriptures *daily*. As long as these new ideas fell within the truth of God's Word,

73

they could embrace the words of the teacher. In fact, this method of thinking is why our mission organization was named The Berean Way. We teach others how to take all kinds of ideas and view them through the lens of Scripture to determine Truth.

I implore you to use the very same process with me and consider these ideas only if they can be verified through the Truths of the Bible.

Our Two Identities

With this thinking in mind, I too examined Scripture. Every Biblical figure I researched seemed to live out two different narratives in their story. Maybe God hadn't personally visited them face-to-face like he did with Abram and Sarai, but they seemed to make important decisions by shifting between their two different identities (or names, as it were).

When they lived in their *false identity (or old name)*, even when they made logical choices, they ran into problems. When they lived in their *true identity (or new name)*, even when they made illogical choices (per God's instructions), they experienced supernatural results and many other people were blessed as a result.

You too might be encouraged to discover how the following characters from the Bible were impacted when they lived between their false and true identities. With that in mind, let's revisit these loosely retold Bible stories about familiar individuals with an emphasis on their identity. Notice how the results of their challenging situations were impacted.

Gideon [60] *(lit. cutter down or brave soldier)*

The people of Israel were chosen by God to bear His witness to the rest of the world. This was Israel's true identity. This tiny obscure people were called to be a light to the larger, more powerful nations of the world to show the love of God. God promised that when they obeyed Him, He would protect Israel and provide for all their needs. [61] However, when they chose to live independent from God, like the other nations in their false identities, He would use their enemies and other events in the world to deliver their consequences. [62] Eventually, God brought them back upon their confession and imploring for forgiveness to return to their true identity.

During one of Israel's dark periods of history, rather than living in their true identity, they became afraid and hid in caves—because apart from God they were weak. They became paralyzed from fear and God sent seven judgments against them via their enemies.

Gideon believed he was a cowardly man (in his *false* identity) from an insignificant family of a self-proclaimed *weak tribe*. God responded to all of Israel's prayers by sending the angel of the LORD. He appeared to Gideon and proclaimed, *The LORD is with you, mighty warrior* (identifying Gideon with his true identity.)

> I always believed God was being sarcastic by calling Gideon a *mighty warrior* because he mostly acts like that of a weak, insecure man through much of this account!

Gideon brought up Israel's recent difficult history *(false id)*. God wasn't interested in discussing the past. He never is. Instead, He focuses on the future and seemed to imply, *you called. I'm here. Let's go.*

The first thing God wanted to do was to remove the sin in the camp. He challenged Gideon's false self-perception and commanded him to obey (acting in his true identity.) Although confused and reluctant, Gideon cut down the community's giant wooden phallic idols and used them to offer a sacrifice to God *(true id)*. He obeyed *(true id)* but did this at night (scared in his *false id*) when no one would see him. Ten men followed him *(true id)*, knowing that this act could possibly cost them their lives *(true id)*.

The next morning an angry mob set out to kill him. I imagine Gideon telling God, *"I knew it! I told you they would kill me (false id)"* A wise man intervened *"Why do we need to defend Baal after he was attacked? Let Baal defend himself."* The community agreed, the mob dispersed, and Gideon was unharmed *(true id)*.

When we move in obedience within our true identity, God brings results we would not normally expect.

The story goes on. Gideon's leadership is littered with frustrating moments *(false id)*. But it all seemed to come together when 32,000 Israelites committed to follow Gideon to deliver Israel *(true id)*. Finally, we see obedience from God's *mighty warrior*.

Israel finally got their momentum back as motivation and excitement filled the air. Then God revealed His battle plan—Gideon was to disband the army he had just assembled and narrowed it down to three groups of 100.

Wait, what?

And each man was to be armed with a trumpet, torch, and clay jar.

You have got to be kidding!

They were to blow the trumpet, break the jar, hold the torch and let God fight the battle *(true id)* for them.

Could you have come up with a worse war strategy?

The scattered nation of Israel somehow chose to obey this *mighty warrior.* God won the war for them and delivered the nation from their enemy.

The Lord brought freedom to His people through a series of unorthodox events led by the most unlikely hero, Gideon—God's *mighty warrior.* When he listened and obeyed the Lord, God used him *(true id)* to overcome Israel's enemies and bring freedom to the nation after years of captivity.

> Israel was also reminded they were not living in their true identity, but that is another story for another time.

Unfortunately, Gideon embraces his true identity on a few occasions. He overcompensates his cowardness *(false id)* with an uncontrollable temper *(false id)*. He later murders a number of his own people *(false id,* then creates a golden idol out of the spoils of war *(false id* which the Israelites end up worshiping after he dies.

It's easy to question why Gideon doesn't remain in his true identity after experiencing first-hand the amazing ways how God works when he is in obedience. But then I look at my own life, see a similar pattern of self-reliance on my false identity and realize how I was trained through years of deception.

Jonah [63] *(lit. dove or deliverer of peace)*

Few stories in the Bible are as confusing as this one. The Ninevites were one of the most wicked people groups the world has ever known. And Jonah, God's prophet, hated them!

Yet God had compassion on them and sent Jonah to give a message to their king that after 40 days, Nineveh will be annihilated. Jonah knew if they repented, God would relent His judgment. So Jonah, wanting them to be destroyed and acting in his false identity, fled in the opposite direction. God eventually got Jonah to Nineveh in a strange story using a giant fish. Reluctantly, yet in obedience through his true identity, Jonah delivered God's message. The Ninevites repented and begged God to save them rather than destroy them. He did. The Ninevites were spared His wrath and one of the greatest miracles in the Bible was recorded.

Jonah, then resorting back to his false identity, stormed off in anger, saying, *Since You didn't kill them, please take my life away from me.* He hiked up a hill above the city to look down over them and pout. God gave him temporary shade from the unbearable heat which made Jonah very happy. Then God took it away, and Jonah bitterly complained, *I'm so angry (about the shade being taken away and the deliverance of the Ninivite) I wish I were dead.* Strangely, the story ends right there.

Jonah reminds us of the freedom God gives us to embrace or reject His calling in our lives. Jonah experienced how God used him in his true identity and could have celebrated with God and sought out other opportunities to bring freedom to others. Instead, Jonah chose to return to his false identity.

Unfortunately, not everyone who experiences the success of living out their true identity chooses to embrace it. Jonah sadly chose to remain in bondage.

King David [64] (lit. beloved)

God's identity for King David was "a man after His own heart." [65] When living in his true identity, King David led the nation of Israel to some of their greatest victories and even today is their most celebrated historical leader.

One time the king took his focus off his true identity and uncharacteristically stayed behind while his armies were at war. He stood on his balcony and watched Bathsheba, the beautiful wife of a friend, bathe.

You know the story. King David is filled with lust and uses his position of power to manipulate a married woman. She gets pregnant, which causes his world to spiral out of control. Fear, anxiety, guilt, and shame asked for control of his life, and he handed it over.

King David unsuccessfully attempted to frame Bathsheba's husband, an innocent man. After that failed, he manipulated his army in the middle of a war to cover up his shame. Bathsheba's husband was finally betrayed and killed, and King David was now cleared to marry Bathsheba.

David thought he was finally free and that no one would ever know. All the evidence was gone, right? However, when you give a foothold over to fear, anxiety, guilt and shame, it will take control of your life and you cannot escape it on your own.

God sent His prophet Nathan to tell David a story about a rich man who lacked nothing but stole a poor man's only sheep from him just to have a party. David, in his false identity still overwhelmed by fear, anxiety, guilt, and shame, exploded in rage when he heard the end of the story: "That rich man should die!"

Nathan confronted David, "That rich man is you!"

Just like that, David recognized his sin as it was revealed in the light of God's truth. He now had a choice to make. David allowed himself to be broken by confessing and giving control of his life back to God. The power of false identity was immediately destroyed. He was forgiven and returned to his true identity as *a man after God's own heart.*

Unfortunately, there were many consequences that resulted from this that lasted for years and ultimately broke up the nation that David had unified. But he was forgiven by God and made free again.

The Apostle Paul [66] *(lit. small or little)*

The Apostle Paul was the son of Zealots, a group of Jews dedicated to removing the Roman occupation and ushering forth God's future Kingdom. As an Jewish leader, he passionately and faithfully served God (or so he thought) by imprisoning all followers of Jesus. And he was quite successful at it.

His birth name was Saul (lit. desired) but it appears he later changed it to Paul after he started to follow Jesus.

Paul described his false identity in the form of a powerful and impressive synopsis:

If any try to throw around their pedigrees to you,

remember my résumé—which is more impressive than theirs. I was circumcised on the eighth day—as the law prescribes—born of the nation of Israel, descended from the tribe of Benjamin. I am a Hebrew born of Hebrews; I have observed the law according to the strict piety of the Pharisees, separate from those embracing a less rigorous kind of Judaism. Zealous? Yes. I ruthlessly pursued and persecuted the church. And when it comes to the righteousness required by the law, my record is spotless [67] . . . I am a Jew, born in Tarsus in Cilicia. I was raised here in Jerusalem and was tutored in the great school of Gamaliel. My education trained me in the strict interpretation of the law of our ancestors, and I grew zealous for God, just as all of you are today. [68]

He later described his true identity in a couple short and humble statements:

Though I am free and belong to no one, I have made myself a slave to everyone, to win as many as possible. [69] **and** For to me, to live is Christ and to die is gain. [70]

He went from one who enslaved free people (his

false identity), to voluntarily enslaving himself (true identity) to Jesus so those in bondage could be made free. In fact, he wrote the book of Philippians with the underlying theme that Followers of Jesus can always be free, *especially* at the pinnacle of persecution, imprisonment, and even death.

God used Paul, one of the Bully's most powerful bullies, to become Jesus' most influential servant leader. Now that is a powerful example of a changed life due to understanding his true identity!

Philemon [71] *(lit. affectionate or one who kisses)*

This short one-chapter book of the Bible is easy to pass over by the casual reader, but it is quite profound. It invites us into very relevant and personal circumstances involving hurt and forgiveness.

Philemon is a fellow Christian who came to follow Jesus because of Paul's influence. However, Philemon was greatly harmed when his slave, Onesimus, ran away.

While in prison, Paul met and led Onesimus to a similar relationship with Jesus. They discovered their mutual relationship to Philemon, and Onesimus had a difficult decision to make. In his old identity of fear, anxiety, guilt, and shame he could continue to run. But everything changed when he learned who Jesus said he was, and his fear was exposed. With Paul's guidance he was ready to do the right thing: return in humility back to his former owner. Can you even imagine?

In the book, we learn that Paul highly respected Philemon because of his love for others. As a result, Paul writes this letter to his old friend Philemon and appeals to his true identity. Rather than focusing on past behaviors and cultural issues like fairness and justice, Paul draws both of their attention to the future. Maybe this is the reason why he was supposed to be away from you for this time: so that now you will have him back forever—no longer as a slave, but as more than a slave—as a dear brother. Yes, he is dear to me, but I suspect he will come to mean even more to you, both in the flesh as a servant and in the Lord as a brother.

How would these two men respond when they met up again? The Bible is intentionally silent about how this all came together. But based on what we understand about these two men, I believe there was a God-honoring result from their reunion because they realized that freedom can only come by living in their true identities. Imagine the never-ending impact this had on their community when they were reunited!

Dumbo *(lit. dumb-o)*

Please indulge me on this one. I realize Dumbo is not a Bible character, but I can't think of a better example of identity discovery and transformation than Walt Disney's personal favorite movie.

Jumbo Jr. was given the cruel nickname of Dumb-o, who was delivered to a mom who was living in captivity at the circus. He was created in a unique and special way, unlike any other elephant before him, with his gigantic ears.

The world he grew up in was harsh. From the beginning Dumbo was treated poorly by his fellow elephants and by the rest of his circus community.

Because everyone told him he should be ashamed of his uniqueness, he learned to live in fear, anxiety, guilt, and shame. Ironically, Dumbo was even bullied by a child with large ears, which set off a chain of events that separated him from his only support, his mom.

Timothy Q. Mouse, with his gentle tiny voice, embraced Dumbo's uniqueness and tried to make him feel special. Dumbo wanted to believe, but the voices around him were too loud. Rather than embrace his true identity, Dumbo believed in the power of a magic feather but that eventually failed as well.

Left with no other alternative, Dumbo finally embraced his true identity and became the hero of the circus. The uniqueness of his large ears was now embraced by his community. He was freed from his fear, anxiety, guilt, and shame and literally soared around the circus in his true identity. He became completely *Alive & Free*.

I could go on and on. We could discuss any other Biblical character from Abraham to Moses, Samson to King Saul, Nehemiah to Peter, Matthew to John and discover the vast differences in their individual lives during those times when they lived between their false and true identities.

Now is the Time

What about you? God has clearly patterned this

idea that He created you with a unique identity and He only views you through that lens.

Simultaneously, the Bully fights against Truth and created these false identities to try to convince you to lose hope and settle into a demoralized life.

Your Creator's love for you gives you the freedom to choose in which identity you are going to live the next chapter of your life. Thankfully, He is not concerned about your past, only your future. So what is holding you back?

If someone were to memorialize your life story years from now, would today be the day when you started to live in your true identity?

6

Embrace Your Identity

> "Give them minds ready to receive wisdom and revelation so they will truly know You. Open the eyes of their hearts, *and let the light of Your truth flood in.* Shine Your light on the hope You are calling them to embrace. Reveal to them the glorious riches You are preparing as their inheritance. Let them see the full extent of Your power that is at work in those of us who believe, and may it be done according to Your might and power."—Paul [72]

The idea of you having a unique, God-given identity might be new to you, but it's certainly not new to the Bully. He has been busy preparing for the day you might learn of your true identity and who you really are. He can't prevent you from discovering God's unique name for you, so he has been working to remove any possible excitement or enthusiasm if you were to discover what it is. This is brilliant planning, because in the event that you learn who God says you really are, you will already be prepared to shut that down and quickly return to your false identity.

It's important to understand that we were conditioned from birth to listen to the Bully and we have learned to accept his words as normal. Scripture tells us this current world belongs to him for a short time, but we belong to God. That truth gives us a position of authority, but we often don't believe it. [73]

During an argument, you might be asked out of frustration, *who do you think you are?* The intent of that aggressive question would be to get you to challenge the foundation of your position in the dispute you are having. If you believe your foundation is shaken, then you can lose confidence in what you are standing for.

The Bully asks us that question all the time while quickly reminding us to respond with our false identities of fear, anxiety, guilt and shame.

But that isn't going to work on you as it has in the past, because God has opened your eyes and is leading you towards freedom through your real identity.

Accusation and Deception

The Bully has only two weapons: *accusation* and *deception*. Christians seem to really struggle with this concept because we have been told by the Bully for our entire lives that we do not have control over our actions *and we believe him!* Our bad choices are then blamed on other people, circumstances and environments.

We listen to the wrong voice. We receive bad advice from the wrong voice. We make poor choices from the bad advice from the wrong voice. Then we blame someone else when things go wrong.

The Bully can't touch you nor control you. All he can do is yell, make demands, and threaten us through his lies. Then he waits until we listen, submit and obey his untruths because that is how he has trained us to think.

It doesn't have to be this way!

In the heat of the moment, it's true that accusations and deceptions sound scary and appear intimidating, but the truth is always the best way to counter those lies. Always!

The problem comes when we don't actually believe the Truth because we don't know the author of Truth. The wrong voice has always told us that the Truth can't actually be defined, it isn't clear or it doesn't exist.

The Bully's master deception formula is simple yet effective and it looks something like this:

1. The Bully is committed to keep us from even knowing we were given a personal, true identity.

    but if that is discovered . . .

2. The Bully is committed to keeping your personal, true identity hidden from you.

    but if that is discovered . . .

3. The Bully has been grooming you to hate your personal, true identity (just in case you make it this far). In fact, he will convince you to believe that it is actually your greatest weakness!

The first stage is obvious. We don't know what we don't know. The more the Bully can keep the truth hidden from us, the more he can control us. He has been very successful at keeping most Christians here for the majority of their lives.

Once you learn you have a true identity, the Bully initiates the second stage and will make a tremendous push to remind you of your false identities. He will try to keep filling you with fear, anxiety, guilt, and shame—but only if you let him. He will bring up your past and remind you of who you used to be. He will yell and scream and try to distract you from seeking your true identity. Sadly, most Christians who do actually get to this stage will not move forward to freedom.

You can plan on encountering spiritual warfare at a whole new level of intensity here. The Bully will create doubt and discouragement with the hope that you will eventually quit your pursuit of the Truth (like you have so many times in your life). He will constantly remind you of your past failures to keep you drowning in guilt.

The Bully needs you to look backwards. If your eyes are focused behind you, you can't see what is coming up ahead, and you will stumble along. You can't walk in a straight line while looking back.

God wants you to confidently direct your eyes forward, toward the future. Your past is over, and He wants to show you where you are going and prepare you for the obstacles you will face.

The third stage will be uniquely challenging as well. Once you hear the personal name God calls you, you might discover you actually despise that name. You will want to deny it or push it away. The Bully's final hope is to groom you to loathe your true identity and to question God's wisdom. If he can't keep you from discovering the truth, he will try to keep you from accepting and acting on it.

Right Identity, Wrong Reaction

When people describe the moment they first hear the name God calls them, they are often surprised.

They immediately try to explain why their true identity can't be the correct one.

This is the Bully's pattern. When God first whispers something to you, the second voice you hear will be your enemy telling you the exact opposite of what God just told you. And we are experts at hearing the Bully's voice.

Andie, my youngest teenage daughter after she prayed, "God, what is the name you call me?"

God responded immediately: *Justice.*

The Bully's voice's quickly followed God's: "Are you kidding me? No way! How can that be true? Remember, you just watched a TV movie involving a courtroom scene. That's probably what you are thinking about. Besides, do you really want to be a lawyer? Or a judge? Think about how boring it would be to be an attorney sitting at a desk inside a building all day. Or what about that little girl's clothing store just down the street called 'Justice?' Are you supposed to work as a retail clerk the rest of your life selling clothes to young girls and their grandmas? Is there a worse identity you could have been given? Obviously,

God didn't speak to you, and *Justice* isn't your real identity!"

I asked her, "Did you hear anything?"

My *confused* daughter responded, "Not really."

"Nothing at all?"

She hesitated. "A word popped into my mind, but it can't be right."

"What did you hear?" I asked.

"The word was *justice*," she said, "but this is why it can't be true . . ." She then began to emphatically argue why *justice* was the wrong word and couldn't be her true identity. She went on and on telling me how that was a ridiculous name to be called. In fact, it became a little awkward how assertively she argued against that being her identity.

Knowing her well, when I heard *justice*, I immediately thought in terms of social justice, authority, and integrity. This made total sense. Andie may be young, but she is an obvious leader. She is a truth-teller, and the kind of person who naturally fights for the oppressed. I immediately wondered how

God was going to use her to bring change to the less fortunate in new ways that have not been tried before. That is how God works in our personal identity.

The problem was, she had been groomed to believe it was the worst identity for her. From the outside looking in, I couldn't imagine a better description of what I see in her.

Did you see how quickly the enemy took her true identity and calling and changed it into a fear of working a mundane job selling clothes to little girls for the rest of her life?

While she was really struggling with this, I was smiling inside because her out-of-character reaction confirmed even further in my mind how terrified the Bully was of losing her to her true identity.

I'm happy to say the Bully didn't win this battle. Andie has since started to learn how to embrace her name and is on her way to discovering where this will take her. But did you recognize how quickly and forcefully he worked?

Even though you can succeed by hearing God's voice, you can still fail by continuing to obey the

Bully's voice instead. You must be prepared for an attack like this, because it *will* come. It always does.

It can be really disappointing when God names you what you don't want to be called. It is a major letdown to finally discover that God calls you the one thing you don't want to be. That is genius deception from the Bully, isn't it?

Of course, deep down we really do want to be what God has made us to be. But you have been groomed and deceived. You have been programed to react the wrong way to the right identity.

Once you recognize this is happening, you can take steps to correct it. Then you will embrace the name God calls you that leads to real freedom.

My Own Rollercoaster of Discovery

That very first evening at our men's retreat with Jamie, I asked God about my own identity. He impressed on me that I was His *"Fearless Teacher."*

Fearless made sense to me. I have an adventurous spirit and love to travel. I enjoy learning something new and discovering unfamiliar cultures and people.

And I tend to embrace the unknown.

But a teacher?

No way! I thought. *What a horrible name to be called. Teachers don't make very much money and aren't respected as true professionals. Wasn't there a saying that "Those who can't do, teach?" This name must be a mistake!*

Then God took me on a flashback through several events in my life.

I clearly remembered this experience I had long forgotten from when I was a young kid in elementary school. One day in class, the thought came to me that I could be a good teacher. That idea seemed so exciting to me at the time.

God, was that your voice calling me way back then?

But I also remember how that excitement quickly passed, and immediately being a teacher became a ridiculous idea. I was a difficult middle school kid and didn't treat teachers kindly because I didn't respect them. *Why would I ever want to be associated with that profession? No way!* Without even knowing it, I chose to listen to the Bully.

I am not a teacher!

As life went on, I saw myself as a Christian businessman. Businessmen made money and were successful and respected. (At least that was what I chose to believe.) So I accepted the business route for my life instead of teaching. It was settled!

But right after my college graduation, I volunteered to serve as a youth leader and guided a group of young guys through life. I started when they were in middle school, and mentored them through high school, then college, then jobs, then marriage and kids. Today we are now peers, and I am still closely involved in several of their lives.

But that doesn't make me a teacher, right?

I also led a weekly, verse-by-verse men's Bible study for over fifteen years.

Would that be considered teaching?

For the past two decades with The Berean Way organization, I have educated countless people all over the world in a unique way on how to read and study the Bible for themselves. In Africa, they called me *mwalimui,* which I later learned from an internet search means *teacher* in Swahili. I brushed that off, too.

So back to that moment of discovery of *fearless teacher.* I knew what I heard God say, but I wanted to hear something more exciting. So like most, I initially rejected it, only to come around full circle to embrace it.

They say hindsight is 20/20. Today, I look back and laugh at my reluctance to accept His name for me. It was obvious that even in my denial, I have always known my true identity. Now I cherish it. God created me and named me for His purposes.

I am a fearless teacher for God!

Obviously, the areas where I have been most fulfilled in my life have involved teaching. And I shine even brighter when I am teaching in difficult areas of the world where most folks refuse to go. I was groomed by the Bully to reject the very person God designed me to be, and I wasn't truly alive until I embraced my true identity.

No More Deception

You now know what I didn't. The deceptive plans that the Bully uses as he wages war against you have been uncovered.

The enemy has been working diligently to blind you and divert you from the true identity that God has been calling you to all along. The next step will be to learn the lies that you still believe about yourself. Some you will recognize, but others have been hidden from you.

It's time to ask God to take you to the next level.

7

Can I Seriously Hear from God?

"The name of the LORD is a strong tower; the righteous man runs into it and is safe." —King Solomon [74]

"Call to me and I will answer you and will tell you great and hidden things that you have not known." —God [75]

From an early age, I was uncomfortable with the notion of even thinking about asking God to speak to me let alone expecting Him to provide an answer. I was highly impressionable growing up as part of the MTV Generation and the influence that television had on us would greatly shape our future. Late night TV introduced several bad influences and the Church was not immune.

There were many questionable ministry examples that helped create that erroneous impression on me. So-called *TV Evangelists* would confuse and scare me. Jesus warned His followers, "Watch out for false prophets. They come to you in sheep's clothing, but inwardly they are ferocious wolves." [76]

Anyone who claims to follow Jesus with their words, but then counters His message with their actions doesn't invalidate God's truths. They only prove they are false teachers who are not from God. However, the Bully wants us to believe otherwise.

At the time, I thought these people were obviously important because they commanded attention, spoke to large crowds, and had a sizable entourage standing around them on stage. They often reminded their viewers of their importance and acted as if they controlled God and His power like a street performer controls a circus monkey. Although I wasn't old enough to articulate it at the time, they left an unfavorable impression on me.

One said he held the Holy Spirit in his hand and then made a throwing motion at the crowd as dozens of people all simultaneously fell backwards out of their chairs. Another claimed he had God's power to heal people at his disposal by thumping them on the head and pushing them backwards into the arms of men who acted like robots. Some would stand on giant stages with a group of huge, intimidating men standing behind them, like bodyguards looking to start a fight.

They claimed to talk to God, and that He would then tell them what to do.

I couldn't quite understand why *God's people* chose to behave like this. Even as a kid who didn't have a firm grasp on the Bible, I understood that something wasn't right with their words and actions. The problem for me was that I associated the importance of talking with and hearing from God directly with these charlatans and concluded that it wasn't an option for me.

The Bully used those false leaders to convince me that hearing from God was probably a scam. I dismissed the idea of God ever *clearly speaking* to me, especially on a regular basis, because that was associated with the deceptions of those false teachers.

I had to learn much later in my life that just because

someone misrepresents communication with God, doesn't mean He can't nor won't want to regularly communicate with me.

Just Ask

We've been discovering how to live *Alive & Free*. The only way for this to happen is for you to know your true identity—who God made you to be. Only He can tell you who you really are and how you can live this out in the world.

In order for that to happen, you have to hear Him and obey. And you have to believe that God really does communicate with us. He speaks all the time, every single day.

Let's think this through logically. If God created you for a purpose and gave you an identity, He will not hide it. He will not make it difficult to find nor understand. He will not send you through an obstacle course in order for you to earn it. Nor does He require you to endure a certain amount of suffering to be deemed worthy of His grace. You can't earn your identity.

It is His gift to you, and He wants you to be aware of your true identity in order for you to walk with Him in the way He has always intended.

So how can you know your true identity?

It's simple.

Just ask.

That's it!

And He *will* respond. Even to those who do not believe He exists.

Why? *Because He loves you.*

God knew from the beginning of creation He needed to provide a way to bring us back to Him through Jesus. He had to do the work, but we needed to accept it. He can't force closeness on us or that is no longer love.

God's love is something you and I will never fully understand. Love is a precious gift that is both a choice and commitment. It is a choice because you can't force someone to give or accept your love. It is a commitment because love overlooks all disappointment in those it loves.

Think of a mother with her newborn baby. She thanklessly provides for every one of her infant child's needs. Yes, it's not easy, but crying, dirty diapers, and a lack of sleep are just more ways to show her love. And if a real threat ever arises, she would give up everything, even her life, for her child's safety and protection. No one messes with a Mama Bear! This is true love.

There is no greater mystery than God's love for us. This love is revealed in infinite ways (colors, gravity, sunsets, mountains, lightning storms, waterfalls, puppies, forgiveness, smiles, friends, music, to name a few). But it is also revealed through His desire for intimacy with us.

He freely gives His love to you, and He patiently waits for you to receive it. The problem is we are so trained to listen to the voice of the Bully that we don't really know God's voice. The false idea that your identity would be concealed from you or difficult to discover goes against His very character.

Why would God work so hard and sacrifice so

much only to go silent after our relationship is restored with Him? He will never make us walk alone.

> Be strong and courageous. Do not be afraid or terrified because of them, for the Lord your God goes with you; He will never leave you nor forsake you. [77]

God isn't silent, but He doesn't talk like the Bully, either.

The Bully's Voice vs. God's Voice

An out-of-control child yells and screams to get what it wants. A guilty person verbally attacks and accuses to distract from their indiscretions. A violent protestor hides their face, joins a mob, and commits acts of violence and vandalism against people and property. A terrorist uses weapons and explosives to maim and kill innocent people—even children.

None of these actions bring credibility nor peace, but they are clear pictures of how the Bully speaks and acts.

On the other hand, a wise counselor asks questions before offering words of wisdom. An understanding friend will listen patiently before speaking. An enlightened mentor will wait and observe rather than react to chaos around him.

Consider these Scriptures of wisdom advising us on godly communication:

> People who despise advice are asking for trouble; those who respect a command will succeed. [78]

> A fool takes no pleasure in understanding, but only in expressing his opinion. [79]

> The way of a fool is right in his own eyes, but a wise man listens to advice. [80]

> A soft answer turns away wrath, but a harsh word stirs up anger. [81]

> Be angry and do not sin; do not let the sun go down on your anger. [82]

> Know this, my beloved brothers: let every person be quick to hear, slow to speak, slow to anger; for the anger of man does not produce

the righteousness of God. [83]

The Bully is always yelling lies at us. Like a small child, he demands immediate attention at all times. When we don't listen, he starts accusing us and brings up our past. If he can't convince us that way, we can expect him to try and rattle our emotions to get our attention.

Contrast that behavior with God, who waits patiently for us for come to Him. He might send us a little nudge to get our attention, but He is patient. He will wait for us.

He does not compete with the Bully. Ever! It is not a battle between them.

The book of 1 Kings presented God's voice this way:

> The Lord said, "Go out and stand on the mountain in the presence of the Lord, for the Lord is about to pass by." Then a great and powerful wind tore the mountains apart and shattered the rocks before the Lord, but the Lord was not in the wind. After the wind there was

an earthquake, but the Lord was not in the earthquake. After the earthquake came a fire, but the Lord was not in the fire. And after the fire came a gentle whisper. When Elijah heard it, he pulled his cloak over his face and went out and stood at the mouth of the cave. Then a Voice said to him, "What are you doing here, Elijah?" [84]

God's voice wasn't in the great and powerful wind, the earthquake, nor the fire. Elijah had to wait for the gentle whisper to hear Him.

Remember that God is pursuing you, but He won't make you pursue Him back. Instead, He reminds you in different ways, and waits for you to make the effort to reach back out to Him. He really wants to talk to you! We call that prayer, but essentially that is just having a conversation with God.

> I highly recommend you read through the rest of this chapter once, and then re-read it and respond at your own pace. It's that important!

Prayer Is Talking to God

Prayer is simply talking to God in the context of a

personal relationship. There are no necessary formalities. You don't need to get caught up in or be concerned about the right time, location, or correct words to say. Remember the wisdom from my ten-year-old daughter, who shared her faith with her friend? It is always the right time and location to express to your Creator what's on your mind.

For my journey, I start by asking God to clear away any distractions. I ask Him to silence the voice of the Bully. I ask that all things that are not from God (such as anger, doubt, worry, confusion, guilt, anxiety, fear, shame, pride, jealousy, etc.) will be completely eliminated from my heart and mind so that I can hear His voice.

I acknowledge who He is and what He has done in my life. I ask Him to join my heart and mind with His heart and His mind. This is also what He wants! Because my perspective is so narrow, I go to my Creator and ask Him to expand my understanding of anything He wants to communicate to me.

Are You Ready?

Let's talk to God right now by asking Him, *"What*

false identities do I call myself that are lies and not true?"

Write down everything that comes to mind. Don't think about it nor question it, just write.

After you are finished, symbolically give that list over to Jesus.

What did He do with it? Write that down what you experienced and how that made you feel.

Now comes the most exciting part.

Ask your Creator, *"What is the name You call me?"* or *"Who do You say that I am?"*

Write down the first thing that comes to your mind. It could be a word, a phrase, an image, a song—anything. Don't question it or try to process yet. You are simply documenting what you heard.

Two Voices

Remember that when God speaks truth, those initial words you hear will be from the Lord. Expect that immediately following will be lies from the Bully in direct opposition to what God just revealed to you. This will be the pattern you will experience going forward.

How can you know the difference between the voices?

God's words are true. They will never contradict the Scriptures. They will bring glory to Jesus. They might exhort or challenge you, but they will never condemn you. They will take you forward and reveal to you who God created you to be.

Once you start to hear Him, you might even recognize His voice. Don't be surprised if it's not new and is distantly familiar. Remember He has always been there talking to you, but He doesn't yell or demand attention like the Bully.

When it happens you might think, *God, so that was You? I've heard Your Voice before, but I didn't realize that was You speaking to me.*

The Bully, on the other hand, speaks lies. His words will tell you what you can't do. They will condemn and discourage you. They will remind you of your past and destroy any hope for your future.

Now go back and read the word(s) God gave you

117

to write down. They should trigger something inside of you. They might even make you mad, but that is OK. Remember we are going through a process of discovery. You'll probably realize that deep down you have known about your true identity all along.

Now write out your additional thoughts or questions.

If you did not hear anything, do not be alarmed nor discouraged. Keep reading. Please know this is not uncommon, and we will address this in the next chapter.

God Will Speak

Hearing God's voice might be challenging at first, but once you understand how to hear Him, you will want to share your discovery and see others experience this kind of intimacy with God. This is true discipleship.

During one of my travels, my team and I were teaching in a tiny village in southern India for several days. The closest hotel for us to stay in was nearly an hour away. It was a miserable drive each way every day on terrible roads. Sometimes when things are challenging, we believe the lie that God *must not be in this situation with me.* Believe me, that thought crossed our minds!

But at the conclusion of our three-day conference, an older woman came up to us, her eyes filled with tears of joy. She thanked us for being the answer to her prayers, because ten years ago she started praying that God would bring a group of leaders to teach her people how to read the Bible. Without even knowing about us, she patiently waited and never gave up hope that He would send us to this tiny village in the middle of nowhere.

If God can be moved to action for a small group of people in an unknown village, you can trust He is pursuing after you as well.

God's desire is to talk with you daily through your true identity. He has given you a name that He calls no one else and you are more precious to Him than you can possibly comprehend.

He wants to share His heart and guide you through your daily decisions, from the mundane to the very important ones.

Once you begin, nothing can hold you back from thriving in your relationship with Him.

Are you ready to do this?

Let's hear from God!

8

What If He Didn't Say Anything to Me?

"Be still, and know that I am God; I will be exalted among the nations, I will be exalted in the earth." —God [85]

You prayed. You confessed. You waited.

But God said nothing. No words. No phrases. No images.

There was complete silence.

Now what?

Does silence mean you're doing something wrong?

Remember, the Bully is looking for and creating opportunities to be the voice you hear. Fear, anxiety, guilt, and shame are probably creeping back in. You're likely thinking, *What's wrong with me? Why is God not talking to me?*

If you don't hear anything, remember that God doesn't hide from you. He is constantly communicating with us, even when we are not aware:

> The heavens declare the glory of God; the skies proclaim the work of his hands. Day after day they pour forth speech; night after night they reveal knowledge. They have no speech, they use no words; no sound is heard from them. Yet their voice goes out into all the earth, their words to the ends of the world. [86]

Barriers to Hearing from God

There are many barriers and lies that can hinder you from hearing His Voice. Here are a few important ones.

Sin

If you have unconfessed sin, then you need to deal with it right away.

Stop what you are doing and confess (tell the truth). God wants you to be real and raw. Talk to Him. Tell Him everything!

Are you mad or hurt? Are you afraid He will not hear you or respond? That's OK. He can take it! He promises to forgive you instantly and free you so you can move forward. There is no shame in confession—only freedom. He is the God of truth! Shame is a false identity the enemy uses to scare you and keep you distracted. But be encouraged: If you feel overcome by shame, this is a sure sign that you are heading in the right direction and the enemy is afraid of you discovering freedom. Ask God to remove your shame, and He will replace it with freedom.

False Identities

Sometimes we might approach God by just going through the motions without really seeking His heart. Maybe you don't really expect Him to talk to you, because you know you are not worthy.

Again, stop what you are doing and confess (tell the truth). God wants you to be real and raw. Talk to Him. Tell Him everything!

Do you ever say the following to yourself: *"God could never forgive a person like me"* or *"I'm only deserving of punishment, not worthy of His attention"* or *"I hate myself—how could God even care about me?"* Ask Him to identify those false identities which are barriers that impede you from moving forward. Then ask Him to tell you names that He calls you.

Intent

Consider whether you're expecting God to say something that He isn't going to say. Or maybe you're looking for Him to declare what you want to hear. Instead, we should ask Him to tell us what *He* wants us to know.

Stop what you are doing and confess (tell the truth). God wants you to be real and raw. Talk to Him. Tell Him everything!

We have been groomed to think we know what we are going to hear before it is even said. Be aware that confession isn't telling God what you expect Him to say. God doesn't work that way. Ask Him to

126

remove your false expectations. It is exciting and freeing for you to discover the truth from Him (He knows better than you do anyway!)

Distraction

This is the issue I struggle with the most. If there are too many things going on in your brain, you can't focus. Distractions can come externally, from our immediate surroundings, and internally, from our minds working overtime.

Stop what you are doing and confess (tell the truth). God wants you to be real and raw. Talk to Him. Tell Him everything!

Change your location. Take a walk. Get into your car and shut the door. Ride a bike to the park, take a hike in the mountains or walk along the beach. God can take those distractions away and free you from the noise around you. Pray for God to immediately silence the Bully and his distractions. Embrace the silence and take several deep breaths. Ask God to speak to you, and to open your ears.

So right now, share with Him what is on your heart. Truthfully. Don't worry about what you think

He wants to hear. Tell Him exactly what you are feeling and why that makes you afraid. Then wait. And listen.

Freedom Can Only Come from Truth

As we dive deeper into the truth, it will become more challenging, if not downright difficult. Please don't take this as a discouragement as it is actually an encouragement. The discovery of your core feelings, emotions, and thoughts can only be worked out with God if you are willing to be honest.

Your conversation might go something like this,

OK, God, you want truth from me? Here you go. My life is a mess, and everything seems to be going wrong for me.

Why?

Because no one really loves me. I am surrounded by people who all seem to want to take me down. If You want honesty, then I am angry at You! If You really loved me, then why would You let all these bad things happen to me? I'm the victim!

That's good. You are starting to be honest with Me.

Why do You sit up there on Your throne and watch me suffer? Don't You love me?

Tell me more. What else do you want to say?

And what are other people going to think? I am trying to be a good Christian, but You are making me look bad with Your lack of involvement in my life.

Why do you feel that way?

I have friends who don't even know You, and their lives are better than mine.

Keep going.

It isn't fair!

What isn't fair?

You don't seem to be concerned about me like You are with everyone else.

Why do you really feel that way?

Because I'm afraid!

What are you afraid of?

I'm afraid YOU DON'T LOVE ME!

YES! That's the kind of truth I was looking for. Now that you are being honest with Me, we can work on the core issues. Here is what I want you to know . . .

Perhaps you feel this kind of dialogue is disrespectful. Well, isn't that part of our problem? We feel like we need to gently tell God what He wants to hear rather than having the freedom to be real with Him. Honesty is how He gets to our core issues.

God will not speak to you in your false identity. He can only deal in truth.

This was just an over simplified example showing how the process of being truthful can look like when you honestly talk to God. Remember He knows all of these things, including your true feelings. The point is that you need to talk them out with Him and let Him respond with His words. You need to speak to Him in truth before you can hear His truth for you!

King David, whom God called *a man after his own heart* [87] prayed earnestly and honestly like this:

> How long, O Eternal One? How long will You forget me? Forever? How long will You look the other way? How long must I agonize, grieving Your absence in my heart every day? How long will You let my enemies win? [88]

What If You Still Don't Hear Anything?

Be patient. Silence is not a curse.

We have become experts at hearing the voice of the enemy and listening to the world and ourselves. It takes a little more effort to learn to hear God speak. Remember that God's intention is to draw us close to Him. He wants intimacy with us.

He will use this time of silence to teach you to slow down and become a better listener: For God alone, O my soul, wait in silence, for my hope is from him. [89]

God can also use this time to help you process with Him and confess anything you need to tell Him. Listening and confessing go together like a hand in glove.

Silence is not a punishment. Sometimes it is the very thing we need, and believe it or not, God speaks through the silence. It can be a time to wait, rest, and relax our minds. It is a Sabbath. There is no timeframe, but you might need to experience silence so that you can really hear what God wants to say.

Do not allow discouragement to intimidate you. It is only and always from the Bully!

There are times when I do not hear anything. I have to remember that successful relationships are not based on instant answers. Rather than allow myself to be dejected, I will wait and listen longer. Sometimes, I take that time of silence to talk and let God hear from me.

I once asked three friends if they wanted to try something new. They didn't know Jesus but agreed to go along with me. We all prayed and asked God to individually speak to us. Two of them shared what they heard. The third confided he had heard nothing. I expected him to be discouraged, but he took it as more of a challenge. He spent the rest of the week asking God to open his ears to hear Him speak. He spoke with God every day, seeking His words. The next time we met, he explained that he was learning to know God's voice and believed he felt he was to take a more active leadership role in a certain group. So he did.

Even though the Bully had groomed him to be discouraged, God used that initial silence to give him an active desire to pursue a relationship with the God he didn't know.

The more time you invest in seeking God, the more you will learn His voice and your conversations will become clearer, deeper, longer, and more meaningful.

God's timing is always perfect. He is never early and never late. Don't give up on this. He wants to use these moments of silence to deepen His relationship with you. Eventually, you will hear God's voice because communicating is part of His character and who He is.

9

It's Time We Learn How to Talk to God

"Yet you, LORD, are our Father. We are the clay,
you are the potter; we are all the work of your hand."
—Isaiah 90

My oldest son, Ranger, spent some time after high school in Central America. The internet communication was spotty at best, but one day I received a cryptic message that he was in trouble. My dad mode kicked in, and I started to think about all the bad things that could have happened to my first-born in the jungles of a developing world country. Panic crept in. I felt my heart begin to race, and it quickly went to full throttle. I cried out to *God, I need to know if Ranger is in serious trouble!*

Instantly, I was filled with peace. God let me know there were no major issues, and my anxiety was taken away. I knew he was safe and I confidently shared this experience with my wife. We could now wait patiently for him to call us with more details once he was available.

I asked, and He answered. Immediately. God told me everything was OK.

Was this normal or a one-time event? I wasn't sure, but I did know my relationship with God went to a much deeper level after this experience. The Creator of the universe was willing and able to communicate to me beyond the limited view I had of Him for so long. I didn't understand all that entailed, but I knew He was taking me to a new level of understanding in our relationship.

A Transformed Perspective

When you start living in your true identity, one of

the biggest changes you will notice will be your transformed worldview. Your perspective of the Creator and His creation will be transformed.

Living in your false identity meant you had to live in constant self-preservation and self-glorification—hence the sayings, *it's a dog-eat-dog world* or *If you want something done right, you have to do it yourself.*

Once you discover who God is and who He created you to be, your understanding of *security* will also change. No longer will you feel the pressure to have to protect and defend your own honor, because the Creator of the universe has got your back. He wants to navigate you through life differently because He has a much broader and complete picture of who you actually are.

Since you no longer have to suspiciously look behind you waiting to be attacked, you are now free to move forward and live the life God directs you to live.

Whether you're like me, and believe you have control over your life, or you believe nothing is in your control and the world is against your every effort, I assure you that God has a different plan.

In Chapter 3, we addressed examples of accepted but false Christian theology that keeps us from moving forward in our true identity. Often times our prayers start with wrong assumptions that unnecessarily hinder us from hearing God.

Truth's We Might Not Realize

The following truths are a powerful and humbling reminder of some of God's qualities. If you embrace them, they can free you to expect more from God in prayer.

Life Isn't Fair

If we're honest, we do *not* want God to deal with each of us fairly. His righteous judgment on our sin would be unbearable. We want our human version of fairness, which means others should be assessed differently than we are ourselves. In our culture, fairness is rarely based on truth.

Fairness does not exist in the natural world. When we compare ourselves, we end up winning or losing, depending on who or what we chose to compare. It is a false measurement leading to false results.

Nowhere in the Bible does it say that we are all given the same starting point, course in life, or even the same finish line. God made you with a unique identity. As a result, He won't treat anyone else exactly like He treats you. Our old tendency to compare with one another is destroyed and replaced with the opportunity for encouragement and freedom towards one another.

True freedom results from the elimination of the expectation of fairness. Pray to be released from the burden of judgment and replace it with His truth.

God Is Just

God's very Name is Holy. [91] There are no exceptions to His character. He shows no partiality.

He does not compare us. He knows how He created you and will judge you according to the unique identity and circumstances you were given. He cannot sin, so He is not subject to bribery, manipulation, lies nor deception. [92] He doesn't get tired, hungry, sleep, or take vacations.

God is not bound by the false standards we often

judge ourselves and others with. But He is just, and His justice demands that sin's consequences must be paid for. That's why His Son was sacrificed for us. [93] Unity with God is only restored in this way, and not because of anything we have done.

Be thankful that He is always just. You can pray gratefully knowing you are free from the responsibility of having to deliver justice yourself.

There Is Only One Team

The Bully demands each of us choose a team, because he wants us divided. He doesn't care what the topic is or which side or extreme position you select. Even a neutral position is taking a position as either side may read into a *neutral* viewpoint as a lack of support for their own team. The Bully works all sides for his own good.

Religious groups usually believe God is on their side, but He really isn't. Joshua was picked by God to lead His people into the Promised Land. After decades of wandering through the wilderness, he came upon a Messenger of God the night before they were going to take possession of the Land.

> He looked up and saw a man standing in front
> of him with a drawn sword in his hand. Joshua
> went up to him and asked, "Are you for us or
> for our enemies?" "Neither," he replied, "but as
> commander of the army of the LORD I have
> now come." Then Joshua fell facedown to the
> ground in reverence, and asked him, "What
> message does my LORD have for his servant?"
> The commander of the LORD's army replied,
> "Take off your sandals, for the place where you
> are standing is holy." And Joshua did so. [94]

Joshua learned his lesson. He believed God was on
Israel's side. Instead, God gave Joshua the opportunity
to choose to be on *God's side.* Even though God had
called His people and promised to deliver them, it was
God's team they were invited to be a part of, not the
other way around.

Jesus said it this way: Anyone who isn't with me
opposes me, and anyone who isn't working with me is
actually working against me. [95]

God is His own team and invites us to join Him. At

no point will you be designated as His leader. At no time will you be the one God follows. Even in choosing obedience and embracing our true identity, we can drift off His team and frequently need to be reminded to join back up with Him at any time.

Pray against the things that divide you from others and ask God to guide you back to His team.

Prayer Is Simple

So how do we put this all together? Remember, prayer is just talking to God. But today, the word *prayer* seems to be used to describe a one-way conversation where we talk *to* God rather than talk *with* Him. There are even preconceived ideas about how, when, where, and even why God can be approached. Scott Mauz writes this about human communication, but it fits perfectly with our mistaken ideas about prayer: "The greatest problem with communication is the illusion that is has taken place." [96]

But what if prayer is much more than giving God a list of things for Him to respond to? What if we need to grow into a level of intimacy with the Lord that we

142

haven't imagined possible?

Over the years, praying and trusting that God would answer my prayer requests came naturally for me. I knew He would listen. But I didn't pray with the expectation that I would hear Him speak back to me.

As a kid, I would pray for people to have a safe vacation or get a good grade on a school exam, or to take away a headache or heal someone from cancer.

I would assess the situation. I would determine what I thought needed to happen. Then I would provide my list and my solution to God. Every once in a while, He would even resolve the issue in the exact way that I suggested. I didn't keep records, but I don't remember my success rate being very high.

Pray for a 'yes' but accept a 'no' was a common church phrase I grew up hearing and saying. For the most part, this was how I talked to God.

As I got older, my requests became more mature and authentic, but the formula basically stayed the same. And I got lots of practice: on trips to the middle of India, hundreds of villagers would line up, waiting for us to pray for them for a variety of things—

including health, marriage, good exam scores for children, and demonic possession. We would spend hours after our evening festivals praying sincerely for every single one of them. Some were healed right away; some took several days or longer. Many times nothing happened. Most of the time, I never did hear the results, but it didn't matter. I was there to love them through encouragement and prayer.

Now that I communicate with God all the time, I anticipate constant feedback, because that is who He is. Do I still present requests to God when I pray? Of course I do! Only now I don't feel the need to try and get His attention so He will listen to me. I am communicating my desires throughout my normal course of our relationship, because we talk all the time.

A Two-Way Conversation

A friend had a young family member who was nearing the end of his battle with cancer. My normal Christian response was to say, *"I'll pray for you."* But what does that really mean?

Do I pray for immediate healing?

Do I pray for courage as they go through this

tragedy?

Do I pray for an opportunity for the Gospel to be shared during this time?

Do I pray they are relieved of their pain and that the medicines work through the wisdom of the doctors?

Do I pray for a quick conclusion or for more time for them to spend with family?

Those things all sound nice and Christian-like, but I really didn't know what they needed, and I wasn't able to ask. So as I prayed I heard God say to me, *why don't you ask Me?*

Oh yeah, that's right, I thought. OK, God, what do you want me to know about this? How should I pray?

Would you believe that He told me what to pray? And it wasn't weird or uncomfortable. In fact, it was practical, yet specific to my friend's unique situation.

I later was able to share with my friend what God had said, and to no one's surprise, it was exactly what his family needed at that time.

Do you realize what this could mean in *your* prayer

life? You can now offer to pray for someone, and also ask God about the specifics of what He wants you to pray about.

Living in my true identity has dramatically changed my relationship with God. I went from making requests for Him to solve obvious problems, to becoming actively involved in His work.

Listen, Obey, and Watch What God Does!

As I began to grow in my understanding of prayer, I began to wonder how these same ideas played out in Scripture. Allow me to retell a familiar New Testament story with this new perspective. [97]

God allowed horrible persecution under the Romans to get new believers of Jesus to go spread the Good News. Instead of being terrified by fear, Philip prayed and asked God what He *wanted him to know* and *wanted him to do.* God responded and told Philip to go to a certain place and meet with a foreigner who was passing through the land. Rather than question or disagree with God, Philip obeyed.

In the meantime, God wanted the Good News of

Jesus to reach Ethiopia, and His plan was to do it through the leadership of the royal family. I believe the Ethiopian Queen sent her treasurer to Jerusalem to meet the promised Messiah. But he was saddened to learn Jesus had been killed. He was returning home to deliver this devastating news, but on his way out of Jerusalem, he stopped along the way to re-read from the book of Isaiah. Jesus had to have been the Promised One, he thought, but He was dead. *Now what?*

That was when God intervened.

In perfect timing, Philip connected with the Ethiopian and was the ideal expert to answer his questions. He was a personal disciple of Jesus who spent time with Him before and after His resurrection. He confirmed that Jesus died, but then rose again to fulfill the very Scriptures the Ethiopian was consulting. Now he was enlightened with the rest of the story. He even asked to be baptized right there in a pool of water on the side of the road. They joyfully parted ways and were sent on to their next task.

Philip was reminded how rewarding it was to hear from God and obey His *seemingly* strange request.

When all hope was gone, the Ethiopian's journey turned from a failure to a complete success in a brief moment of time. And God blessed the people of Ethiopia (and Africa) with the right leadership *through their royal family* to deliver the Good News of a risen Jesus to an unreached part of the world. Nearly two thousand years later, I have even served in ministry alongside the descendants of those early Ethiopian Believers. How amazing is that?

Fantastic stories like this one fill the pages of the Bible. God asked people to do things that went against conventional wisdom but resulted in delivery and freedom from oppression. And He is moving like this every day around the world through the true identities of His followers. You can be a part of stories like these, too!

When we live in our true identity and seek God in prayer, ready to hear from Him and obey, the results He brings about can only be described as supernatural. As I look back, I realize I've experienced this on several different occasions, too. I just didn't know it at the time.

Years ago, I was in the middle of Uganda, at

the end of a ministry trip. I nodded goodbye at my driver and watched him drive his rickety old van away from the jungle spot where he had dropped me off near a tiny village. As I walked into the small, dark grass hut that the locals used for a church, I remember thinking, *why am I here? It's the end of a long trip, and I just want to go home.*

It was hot. And humid. And the bugs were thriving in this stagnant air.

I was tired and ready to head to the airport. After teaching, we all went back outside into the sunshine and fresh air. A few villagers sat around and just stared at me. The language barrier was evident, but many of them returned my smile with a nod.

Why did I accept this last speaking opportunity?

I was hangry (hunger leading me to anger) and there was no safe food I could eat with them. The van that was supposed to pick me up was now almost an hour late. Time seemed to come to a halt.

Next time, I will refuse the opportunity to speak one last time before I leave, I thought.

149

In the middle of my complaining and very poor attitude, a tiny frail woman who had been staring at me got up and slowly walked my way. I'll never forget how her sharp gaze pierced deep into my soul.

She whispered something into my translator's ear and a smile spread across his face. He told me she had some questions. Through the translator, she said, "My husband and sons have died. Because there are no males in my house, everything has been taken away from me. I have no property and no rights. I have nothing left. Is it true what you said about Jesus?"

"Yes. He sent me here to tell you that He loves you."

"No one has ever told me I was loved," she replied. My eyes filled with tears.

She thanked me for being obedient to God's call to come to her little village and tell her this great news. She appreciated my sacrifice to leave the comforts of America just to see her. She said she wanted a relationship with Jesus and asked me to tell her more about how she could know this God who sent me to tell her that He loves her.

I reached across to hug her, and I vividly remember holding onto the bones sticking out of her back and shoulders. Her tears flowed onto my neck and down my back, and she wouldn't let me go. I have no idea how much longer I was there, but it didn't matter to me anymore. *Who really blessed who?* The driver showed up right as we finished our extraordinary interaction.

Two days later, I was back at work in Portland sitting at my desk, still trying to process that experience and the lessons God was teaching me.

I now understood that last-minute invitation to speak at that small village church was God's voice, even though I didn't recognize it at the time. I had responded out of obligation, but it was really because God was working through my true identity. Thankfully, what the Bully intended for evil, God used for good. [98]

Let's Ask Him for Direction

My expanded understanding of prayer has changed everything for me. I used to hope God would work through me, but I didn't really expect Him to talk to me and tell me what He wanted me to do.

Now, I no longer have to go through life like a blind man using God as my guide dog, hoping He will keep me out of the oncoming traffic. My eyes have been opened, and I have purpose and direction that's available to me every day if I seek it. I can know where I am going because He tells me, and I can hear Him.

Jesus told His followers, Don't be like them [idol worshippers], because your Father knows the things you need before you ask Him. [99] How many times have you prayed without really knowing what you were even asking for? Since God knows what you need better than you do, wouldn't it be wise to ask Him what it is you should be asking for?

> Now this is the confidence we have before Him: Whenever we ask anything according to His will, He hears us. And if we know that He hears whatever we ask, we know that we have what we have asked Him for. [100]

When we ask God to reveal what we need, and He tells us what He wants us to pray, it will always be answered. If we pray with this in mind, we are more likely to take part in His will every time we pray!

A Confident Expectation

As my relationship with the Lord has become more real and intimate, my expectation that God will answer my requests has grown. Rarely do I now pray from a defensive or reactionary position—even when I'm experiencing difficult times.

I now pray intentionally. I am free to believe that His results from my prayers will be effective. I don't always do it well, but by living in my true identity, I am directed by the heart and mind of Christ in what I ask and how I pray.

When I prayed out of fear, anxiety, guilt, and shame, it often felt more like I was taking a spin on the Wheel of Fortune. I could hit the jackpot or go bankrupt. It was just a game of chance. Now, rather than hope God will hear me, I approach Him confidently with an understanding of the situation and how He wants me to pray.

I trust that you will experience the same thing. Praying with this understanding is an essential part of becoming *Alive & Free*.

10

Know Pain,   Know Gain

"But think about this: while we were wasting our lives in sin, God revealed His powerful love to us in a tangible display —the Anointed One died for us."
—Paul [101]

"Then you will know the truth and the truth will set you free." —Jesus [102]

Now comes the *real* challenge as God doesn't deal in partial truths.

He wants to strip away everything that keeps you from having true intimacy with Him. That means *everything!*

God will speak truth to you, but He expects you will speak truth back to Him. This is where it all begins. To deal in truth means to address your every shortcoming head on. Please stick with me on this, because you have come too far on your journey to not become completely *Alive & Free.*

So where do you go from here?

Confession and Repentance

These common *Christianese* terms may be familiar, but do you really understand what they mean? You might be surprised at how challenging and freeing these essential practices are to the transformation process.

Confession is *simply telling the truth to God and agreeing with Him about your current situation.*

It involves the stating of the facts and detailing your involvement. Declaring *I'm sorry* is what you say after you have been caught in the act of doing something wrong. *I'm sorry* is only a deflection off the real issue and does not bring any real change.

Repentance is *listening to what God wants you to*

do, and then responding with obedience.

You may have heard it defined as stopping, turning around completely and heading the opposite direction, but it is much more than that. Repentance involves making immediate changes to your life based on what God has instructed you to do.

Without confession and repentance working together, there can be no change.

Exposing Darkness to Light

Immediately after learning my true identity, I found I wasn't completely free. I had new purpose, passion, and vision, but I was still anchored down. I wanted to be released to become unquestionably *Alive & Free* so I committed to the process to do whatever it took.

I did not live in my false identity anymore, but my dark past had to be exposed to the light. The Bully tried to convince me that this would be a bad thing. He wanted me to remain hopelessly mired in fear, anxiety, guilt, and shame. He yelled and screamed to keep me in bondage.

However, I knew God promised me freedom by

revealing then removing those areas of past bondage. I committed to the process of confession and repentance, no matter what it took. This was a big step as I knew I would become exposed, uncovered, and vulnerable.

But this was the new and true me. I believed it was safe to confess it all to God, because He knew the real me and loved me anyways. His love is not based on what I do, but rather who He is, what He has done for me, and who He created me to be.

I had reached a point where I was ready to dive deeply into the next stage of my journey in this personal relationship with God. Those dark secrets of my past had to be exposed and dealt with in truth. But I really didn't know what to do.

So I asked God, *what do you want me to know about this particular sin?*

Then I listened. Sometimes He would speak or ask me a question.

Other times, there was silence and I would wait.

In order to be released from my false identity, I started by confessing small, obvious shortcomings that He brought to my mind. Rather than feel ashamed, I felt freedom. Different burdens literally removed different volumes of weight off my shoulders.

For the next nine (often painful) months God lovingly worked through my past secrets and false identities. At least one day per week, usually Saturdays, I would leave the house early in the morning and walk for six to ten miles. It wasn't uncommon for me to spent three hours or more on these walks.

I asked God to open my eyes and ears, and to speak to me. I wouldn't hear an audible voice, but I have learned to tune into His impressions. God often speaks to me through questions that seem to pop into my mind. He would reveal each area of sin in my life, like exposing a room behind a hidden door full of garbage. I didn't realize was how many secret compartments I had constructed over my lifetime and how much junk I was storing up.

When I asked Him the next week, God would bring up something new I had long forgotten about. So I would confess and ask God to reveal when that specific sin (such as jealousy, anger, or lust) first entered into my life. He took me all the way back to that first memory, and I would then give everything about that event over to Him.

I prayed, *Jesus, you have paid the consequences for that action in my past. Please take away any stronghold that I have given to that event, remove it from my life, and replace it with freedom to focus on the future. Thank you for releasing me from my past!*

Week by week, I confessed *(told the truth about)* each sin as it was revealed to me. He took them all away. He didn't relocate them into a different storage location to be brought back out someday in the future. I remembered His promise: I, even I, am He who blots out your transgressions, for My own sake, and remembers your sins no more. [103]

He completely removed those burdens from me. I was amazed at the things He helped me recall but more surprised by how He made them disappear. He had no interest in reviewing my past sins with me because they came from my false identity. He just took them away, never to hold them against me again.

The Last Step of Obedience

On several occasions I thought I had finally confessed everything. Then God would lead me down another hallway in my mind lined with even more doors I had forgotten about. One by one, we went through them all: hallway by hallway, door by door, and room by room. I had no idea of the extent of the rotten garbage that I stored in these hidden compartments over all these years.

One day, there were no more doors to be opened. I had confessed it all. There were no new hallways or rooms that remained. There was nothing left. They had all been exposed. He did it!

Could I really be free? Immediately, the Bully accused me with a vengeance. *How dare you think you could ever be free from sin? Who do you think you are?* he shouted. I started to feel like I should feel guilty.

I was confused and didn't know what to think or do next. I had never heard anyone describe this level of freedom and honestly, I wanted some affirmation from God. So with false humility, I asked God, "What do you want me to know *now*?"

There is something you haven't told your wife, He said.

Immediately, I knew what He was referring to.

"But that was old news and in the past. You and I already dealt with it," I said.

Jeff, you asked me for complete freedom and what I want you to do. I am making it very clear. Go tell your wife. Then we can talk.

"Nope, I don't think I need to. It is irrelevant and ancient history as far as I'm concerned. Nothing good can come out of that discussion anyhow. Besides, I'm now free, right?"

I think I argued with God over the next couple miles of that particular walk. Eventually, I had stated my case strongly enough that it seemed like He should have a good understanding of my position.

I felt like I had done everything I was supposed to and should have felt *Alive & Free* . . . but I wasn't. And I knew it.

The next week, I went on my walk with God and asked Him the same question: "What do you want me to know?"

Did you tell your wife? He asked.

"I am *not* going to do that. I don't see any reason why. I thought we had this resolved last week."

Jeff, you asked, and I am ready to take you forward. But we can't move on until you resolve this.

This dialogue went on for at least six more weeks. I finally gave in. OK, if she initiates the question, I will bring this up. That night Erin and I found ourselves in a rare occasion where we were alone in our living room together. Out of the blue, she looked me in the eyes and asked if there was anything I needed to tell her.

I smiled and said, *nope,* then got up and left the room.

Do you think the Bully wanted to take advantage of this situation? You bet! Guilt attacked me like a tsunami because I had let down God, my wife, and myself . . . AGAIN! The following week I started listening to the Bully, and I accepted the full brunt of his abuse. I was beat up, and just like that, I embraced the false identities of fear, anxiety, guilt, and shame all over again.

Fast forward to my next Saturday morning walk. For some reason, I couldn't wait to talk with Him. He didn't reprimand me.

In an odd way, it felt like God was actually trying to help me free myself. The issue wasn't a current behavior that needed to be dealt with; it was a matter of obedience and telling the truth. *Jeff, you need to trust me on this. I want you to want to be free. Go tell your wife.*

Since I had proven I wasn't strong enough to carry this out on my own, I texted my wife in the middle of my walk to let her know I had something important to tell her that night, and she needed to ask me about it later. I pushed send and the message was delivered. There was no backing out now.

Evening came too quickly, and we found ourselves alone. "What did you want to tell me?" she asked.

I took in a deep breath and let it out slowly and proceeded to tell her what God wanted me to share.

Don't get me wrong, it wasn't easy for either of us. But I can't begin to tell you how freeing being obedient was for me, and how it took my relationship with the Lord to a much deeper and more meaningful level.

Weeks later, I asked God why He took me through that last process with my wife. He impressed upon me the following response:

> *Two things. You needed to know that obedience to Me brings complete freedom. When you ask, I need you to obey without question. But I also used your situation to deal with issues I am working on in Erin's life. I used you as an example to communicate truths to her that she needed to hear.*

Now I was free! I mean *truly* free!

And this time, I didn't expect God to praise me, because that wasn't what I was seeking anymore.

Not Perfect, Free

The words that immediately came to mind: Humble yourselves before the Lord, and *He will lift you up*. [104] My how that *familiar* Scripture came alive to me!

And just like that, the Bully came yelling at me with his lies: "True freedom isn't really possible. You're only lying to yourself. Do you think you're better than everyone else? You're not worthy of being forgiven. No one could ever be that free! You're just trying to make yourself feel better."

So I asked God to silence the voice of the Bully. And He did! God reminded me again that I really was completely free!

If God declared me free, then who can argue with that? And isn't this why Jesus came? Quoting out of Isaiah, He read,

> The Spirit of the Lord the Eternal One is on Me. *Why?* Because the Eternal designated Me to be His representative to the poor, to preach good news to them. He sent Me to tell those who are held captive that they can now be set free, and to tell the blind that they can now see. He sent Me to liberate those held down by oppression. [105]

While I will never be *perfect* while here on earth, I am supposed to be *Alive & Free*. Everyone is. Including you!

I can guess what you might be thinking. Yes, there is a huge difference between being perfect and being free.

Do I still get tempted? *Yes.*

Do I still sin? *Of course. This morning, in fact.*

But there is a long distance between sinning and living in sin. When I know and live within my true identity, I am free. I no longer have the time, energy nor interest to be tempted like I used to.

Smooth Sailing on Rough Waters

Let me explain it this way. When I lived in my false identity, it was as if I were swimming alone out in the middle of the ocean. Every time I sinned, it was like I was being pulled down, in danger of drowning. The waves became much rougher at different times, but I was always bobbing up and down. Sometimes, it was all I could do to keep my head above water long enough to take another breath before inevitably sinking under the water again. It was exhausting!

Now that I am living in my true identity, it is as if I am on a large ship crossing that same ocean. There are life jackets, and guard rails and warnings when bad weather approaches. The waves may occasionally splash mist on my face, but I am in no danger of them taking me under. When I sin, I may slip and possibly dip my foot into the water. Or on the rare occasion that I fall in, there is always help right there to pull me out, dry me off, and keep me safe. I may not be completely dry for the remainder of this journey, but I am rarely

Alive & Free

drenched for long.

What about you? Are you tired of feeling like you are drowning? Do you want to experience the freedom that can only be provided by your Creator?

Perhaps you think your sins are worse than mine. Maybe they are. Maybe not. But God doesn't categorize what Jesus has already paid for. His gifts of intimacy and freedom are free and focus on your future.

But they can only be fully received when you live in truth. Not partial truth—100% truth! Remember that confession is agreeing with God about your current situation and repentance is obeying what God wants you to do as a result.

I love the wisdom from the parable asking, *how do you eat an elephant? One bite at a time.* Remember, you can't do it all at once, but if you don't start you will never finish.

You too can start your journey to freedom right now. There will be painful times along the way, and it will not happen overnight. But the path is simple: just ask God where to start and what He wants you to do.

Start with the smaller issues that He brings to your mind. Confess then repent each and every one. You will immediately notice the weight of your false identities being removed off of your shoulders and will have wished you started this process sooner.

I assure you, this journey will take you on the road to   the   freedom   you   seek.

11

The Way   Forward

"For all who are being led by the Spirit of God, these
are sons of God." —Paul [106]

God's ultimate agenda is intimacy with you! He
doesn't want more sacrifices, more suffering, or more
rules. He simply wants you to hear His voice and be
follow His direction. [107]

God is patient and will never give up on you. Don't
you think it's time to listen and obey so you can

become *Alive & Free* in Him?

Once I finally committed to the process, it took what seemed like a long time for God to help me work through all of my false identity issues. But He did.

They were removed so that my true identity would shine through. There will always be many unknowns in my future, but I am now living in the present more consistently with the peace of God, which transcends all understanding. [108]

Once you have received your true identity from God and the Bully has been exposed, you now realize his tricks (false identities). Be warned, he won't stop trying to remind you of your past. However, you should now be so excited about your future with God that you will not have time for the Bully and his lies anymore.

The *way forward* (which is how my African friends describe applying a life lesson) could not be simpler, but it might be one of the more challenging steps in this process. The next several months are critical as you learn to live the way God has always intended.

There are no shortcuts, and the following concepts

have to be lived out for you to comprehend what God really has for you. But the benefits make the effort well worth it.

Quality Time

God wants you. And He wants your time.

All of it!

Western cultures often evaluate successes by the number of tasks that are accomplished. But that's not true in successful relationships where quality time is essential for intimacy.

We need to re-learn how to have a true relationship with our Creator and it all starts with spending time with Him. Jesus modeled to us that His number one priority was spending time with His Father.

Not in healing people.

Not even in delivering the message of the Kingdom of God.

His main focus was intimacy with God.

He would break away to have that quality time

every single day:

> But Jesus often withdrew to lonely places and prayed. [109]

> And rising very early in the morning, while it was still dark, he departed and went out to a desolate place, and there he prayed. [110]

> He (Jesus) withdrew about a stone's throw beyond them, knelt down and prayed. [111]

Jesus spent most of His time with God and He knew God's voice. Our desire should be the same. Good communication requires practice. Hearing from God is simply learning how He speaks to you. There are no shortcuts to quality time and you can't save it up like a bank deposit to draw from later when you are busy. You need to invest in that relationship every single day.

Remember, we tend to want answers and results.

God only wants you and your relationship.

We look for measurable facts, but He wants our time.

Faith

The author of Hebrews says, now faith is confidence in what we hope for and assurance about what we do not see. [112] Biblical faith is confidence and assurance, not blind hope. Faith is knowing that God has delivered 100% on every promise He has ever made, and therefore, any of His future promises *will also be fulfilled.* You can always count on Him. Faith is a validated expectation and is completed when two sides come together.

Picture this. It's summertime at a park. A little girl drags her dad over to a picnic table and climbs on top. Nervously, she stands on the edge but faces the middle of the table with her back to her dad. She hears him whisper *"now"* and without looking she slowly tilts her head back and her body falls blindly like she has done many times before. Just when she thinks she might crash to the grass below, she finds herself securely in her father's arms. He was waiting to catch her, but every time she has to be the one to believe enough to lean backwards and release control. That is a picture of Biblical faith.

Having faith in God's promises requires us to

act, often blindly, knowing God will always be there to deliver what He promises us.

Uninformed people often mock a Christian's faith because they think it is a blind hope without any real substance. They call it a crutch for a weaker person who can't deal with reality by themselves. The truth is, faith is based on confidence and assurance in who God is and who He calls us to be.

Here is another thought. It doesn't take any faith to believe a lie. When the Bully tells you that *you can't do something,* where is the faith in that? It's easy to agree with him and do nothing. That isn't faith.

It takes real faith to believe the truth. When God asks you to do something that doesn't make logical sense, it will take real faith to believe and act it out. We see this over and over again with different individuals in the Scriptures.

Ironically, Biblical faith takes strength. A lack of faith is the real crutch. And it's also a weakness.

Did you know there were two things that amazed Jesus during His earthly ministry? The presence of faith and the lack of faith. [113]

Let me leave you with the following truths.

Confession: Telling the Truth

Although this was addressed in the previous chapter, I think it is important to emphasize that God can't work through you in your true identity until you learn to live in truth daily. There is no better time to start than right now. Confession simply means to tell the truth and not just say you are *sorry*.

Any secrets or false identity lies that you are still holding onto will prevent you from experiencing the deep relationship God wants to have with you. If you are angry, sad, frightened, defeated, shamed, embarrassed, lazy, controlling, beaten down, without hope, or just flat out questioning if God even exists, just tell Him. Besides, He already knows all of those things! So tell Him right now.

God will be truthful with you and always responds in love to those who honestly seek Him.

Repentance: Hearing and Obeying

It's easier to hear God than it is to obey. When

God provides you with truth you then need to make changes to alter your thoughts and behaviors to what He tells you is true. That is real repentance.

Hearing and obeying are like two hands clapping. Both must come together to make noise. Otherwise, all you are doing is moving air around.

Two Voices, Two Very Different Messages

Two voices will constantly be communicating with you: God's voice and that of the Bully. Many wonder if they will be able to discern which is which or if they might confuse the two. This lack of confidence leads to confusion. Confusion leads to fear. And fear will keep you frozen in inactivity. Jesus assures us:

> My sheep hear my voice *[more than just listening]*, and I know them *[through a personal relationship]*, and they follow me *[obey with actions]*. [114]

History is in the past, and the Bully will try to draw your attention back to what can't be changed. He wants you to constantly look behind you. Jesus never looked back so He could always see the enemy coming in front of Him. Your freedom enables you to look forward, no longer needing to look behind you.

So how can we distinguish between God's and the Bully's voices? It's actually much clearer than you think. You must understand the intent behind the two messages.

When we stop and focus our attention in order to hear God, the first voice we hear *is* God's. The second will be the Bully trying to counter that truth. It may seem confusing at first, but the actual substance, delivery and timing of both voices are much different from each other.

God's voice:

- is quiet like a whisper
- lifts you up
- asks you to do things that require faith to believe
- introduces you to non-traditional thinking
- values your individuality and creativity
- may persuade you into action that isn't logical
- aligns with what Scripture says

The Bully's voice:

- yells and screams and intimidates
- condemns and tears you down
- brings fear, anxiety, guilt, and shame
- reminds you of your past failures
- works non-stop to convince you that your true identity is false
- is easy and requires no faith to obey
- grooms you to conform to cultural thinking that counters truth
- often leads to inaction using logic

Grace When We Fail

A few mornings ago, I prayed and challenged God to use me during the day.

While in morning traffic, I inched myself along and waited my turn to merge onto an onramp. There was a homeless guy begging on the corner. I considered giving him my unopened protein bar, but immediately, I thought about how inconvenient it would be to dig through my bag that was right next to me in order to find it. The traffic line was long, and I might make someone mad if I stalled everything for a few more seconds. I also saw someone hand him something a few cars ahead of me. *Besides,* I thought, *it looks like many others are already being so generous to him.* So I drove on.

Later that morning, I was walking to a meeting in downtown Portland. An obese man in a wheelchair was taking his tiny lap dog out for a potty break. I watched the dog finish going number two, and then I watched this man really struggle to bend over to pick up after his dog. He couldn't do it. I clearly heard God tell me to help him. But I just kept walking along. I tried unsuccessfully to justify to myself why I needed to be early to the meeting to make a good impression.

Then I waited for a rooster to crow twice. *(Joking, not joking!)*

In a matter of a few short hours, I blatantly ignored God's answering of my request from earlier in the morning.

I prayed. I heard. *But I didn't obey.* This was not the formula for success. Thankfully, God knows this will happen to all of us and He gives us this promise: "If we confess our sins, he is faithful and just and will forgive us our sins and purify us from all unrighteousness." [115]

I confessed and was made free again. Immediately, the enemy tried to use these events to remind me of my failures in the past. He wanted me to feel guilty. But I recognized that is a false identity and embraced God's forgiveness instead.

No one was hurt from my disobedience, but I missed out on an opportunity to be a part of something God was doing. I don't know what that was, or where it could have led to, but there was a lesson to learn.

Did you also notice how much more energy and focus was required for me to *not* obey? Once again, I was reminded of how important it is to keep my eyes focused on who God is and who He created me to be.

The Ride of a Lifetime

All of these Biblical truths we have discovered become worthless if we don't apply them personally. Knowing more doesn't matter if it doesn't cause change in our daily behaviors.

Remember, God sent Jesus to die for your sins so that you could be restored with your Creator. Intimacy with Him is His ultimate goal for you. It is the thread that runs through the entire narrative of the Bible—from the very first page of Genesis through the book of Revelation. Scripture was all written for the purpose of reuniting you with your Creator. Every story and every character invite you into a deeper understanding of God.

From His Word we learn of His unconditional love and His pursuit of us, even though we treated Him like an enemy. True freedom is realized when we choose to accept His love, and we are restored to the intimate relationship He created us to have with Him from the very beginning. That freedom is then lived out through our true identity, given to us by Him.

Your true identity is a gift. It is a unique calling. You can't create it or change it. Nor is it an accomplishment you brag about.

True intimacy with God is what He desires from you more than anything. And it is *very* attainable. However, it is *your* choice!

If you do decide to seek true intimacy with God, strap on your seat belt and get ready for the ride of your life. He will take you to places you didn't know existed, ask you to do things that you will not understand, and reveal to you insights and glory that you could never have imagined without Him.

We have been given the greatest gift of all time: a personal relationship with God through His Spirit and the opportunity to be used by God to change our world. But that event was meant to only be the beginning.

Living in your unique, God-given identity reveals your own exact role is in His master plan.

So are you ready?

Please join me in becoming *Alive & Free*!

Conclusion

As I review this book for the umpteenth time, I am so excited about all that God has taught me through this process. I trust God has been stirring your heart as well to *really* know who He is and who He has created you to be. And I hope you now believe you too can be *Alive & Free!*

If you haven't already done so, take that first step and ask God to reveal Himself to you in a new and real way. He will do that because that is His character.

You will seek me and find me when you seek me with all your heart. [116]

If you are not a follower of Jesus, then pray all He has placed in your heart and ask Him to be your Lord and Savior and to guide you on your new journey moving forward. Welcome to the family!

Talk to Him throughout day.

He will *guide* you.

He will *answer* you.

And He will *give* you all you need to know. But you have to be willing to deal in truth because He does not work in your false identity.

Maybe you still don't know what to say to Him?

> "All things are possible for one who believes." Immediately the father of the child cried out *[to Jesus]* and said, "I believe; help my unbelief!" [117]

Ask God to help your unbelief!

All of us have been deceived and groomed by the Bully for far too long. The answers do not lie within you or me, or with catchy phrases. Popular self-help and positive thinking will not get to the root issue and help you know your Creator and be all He made you to be.

Thank you for taking on this journey with me. It's time for you use that key to unlock your cell one last time, leave that old prison and run towards Jesus to discover your true identity and become *Alive & Free!*

This story is a living project that includes you and is constantly being written. I invite you to join the discussion at alivefree.org.

Questions? Comments? Please feel free to reach out to us at aliveandfreediscussion@gmail.com.

I   truly   bless   God   for   you   -   Jeff

Thank You

I wanted to acknowledge the following people for having the courage and persistence to challenge and push me to make sure this book was completed. I could not have done this without them. To Erin: my smoking hot wife, best friend and confidant, I love you more today than ever before. To my kids: Ranger, Arabella, Andie and Storm, may you become *Alive & Free* through God's unique identity and journey for each of you, both individually and together. To Calli and her wonderful artistic talent that was re-discovered through very difficult circumstances. To Stephanie, the editor extraordinaire who patiently provided me wisdom, insight and guidance, while letting me express myself the best I could. And finally to all those who have contributed their time and energy to help shape this book with their suggestions: my parents, Sam, Jamie, Reid, Ian, Todd, Megan, Eliot, Dana, Aaron, Meghan, Jeff, Kendra, Herb, Brad, Dan, Tim & Lynn, Nicole, Jay, Shana, Tim, Britany, Jeff and Chris. Thank you all very much.

Endnotes

For those of you who want to dig deeper, here you will find references, additional information, personal insights, Bible passages, and more.

---

[1] For more information, I highly recommend you read the book *Finishing Strong* by Steve Farrar. My father-in-law gave me this book 20 years ago, and I still refer back to it today. The sad truth seems to be that a majority of us will not finish our Christians lives deeply committed to the faith that once spurred us on. One of the outcomes of my book is to explain why this is true and what can be done to change it.

[2] Very few people have lived out their faith like Jim Elliot, a Christian missionary martyred by the Huaorani people of Ecuador he was trying to serve.

[3] This is my thesis for the entire book. It is the premise that took me from personal conversations on this topic to actually obeying God's calling to write it out.

[4] John 8:36, NIV

[5] 1 Peter 5:8, NIV

[6] Isaiah 14:12-20, NIV, Ezekiel 28:1-19, NIV

[7] In John 12:31-33, NIV, Jesus prayed right before His crucifixion, "Now

is the judgment of this world; now the ruler of this world will be cast out."

[8] Matthew 4:1-11, NIV

Matthew 13:19, 39, NIV

John 8:44, NIV. 1 Peter 5:8, ESV

Revelation 12:9-10, ESV

[9] 1 Peter 5:8, NIV

[10] John 8:44, NIV

[11] "Fetus to Mom: You're Stressing Me Out!" WebMD. Accessed January 18, 2020. https://www.webmd.com/baby/features/fetal-stress#1.

[12] See the following excerpt from "The Effects of Stress on Your Body." Healthline. Healthline Media, September 29, 2018. https://www.healthline.com/health/stress/effects-on-body#2.

"You're sitting in traffic, late for an important meeting, watching the minutes tick away. Your hypothalamus, a tiny control tower in your brain, decides to send out the order: Send in the stress hormones! These stress hormones are the same ones that trigger your body's "fight or flight" response. Your heart races, your breath quickens, and your muscles ready for action. This response was designed to protect your body in an emergency by preparing you to react quickly. But when the stress response keeps firing, day after day, it could put your health at serious risk. Stress is a natural physical and mental reaction to life experiences. Everyone expresses stress from time to time. Anything from everyday responsibilities like work and family to serious life events such as a new diagnosis, war, or the death of a loved one can trigger stress. For immediate, short-term situations, stress can be beneficial to your health. It can help you cope with potentially serious situations. Your body responds to stress by releasing hormones that increase your heart and breathing rates and

ready your muscles to respond. Yet if your stress response doesn't stop firing, and these stress levels stay elevated far longer than is necessary for survival, it can take a toll on your health. Chronic stress can cause a variety of symptoms and affect your overall well-being. Symptoms of chronic stress include:

- irritability
- anxiety
- depression
- headaches
- insomnia

[13] Isaiah 43:1, ESV

[14] 2 Timothy 1:7, HCSB

[15] Matthew 6:33, ESV

[16] Proverbs 7:1, NIV

[17] Proverbs 12:25, ESV

[18] Philippians 4:6-7, ESV

[19] Psalm 32:5, NIV

[20] Romans 8:1-2, NIV

[21] John 8:36, NIV

[22] Romans 10:11, NIV

[23] The *flesh* refers to our fallen sin nature (literally the unhealthy pursuit to meet our physical urges) which the Spirit of God helps us overcome. The *world* is that part of our culture that opposes God's truth. "As for you, don't you remember how you used to just exist? Corpses, dead in life, buried by transgressions, wandering the course of this perverse world [world]. You were the offspring of the

prince of the power of air [Bully] —oh, how he owned you, just as he still controls those living in disobedience. I'm not talking about the outsiders alone; we were all guilty of falling headlong for the persuasive passions of this world; we all have had our fill of indulging

the flesh [flesh] and mind, obeying impulses to follow perverse thoughts motivated by dark powers. As a result, our natural inclinations led us to be children of wrath, just like the rest of humankind." Ephesians 2:1-3 VOICE

[24] Isaiah 42:6-7, ESV

[25] Psalm 51:5, NIV

[26] Matthew 16:24, NIV; Jesus said this to his closest disciples who were spending all of their time with Him.

[27] Matthew 11:28, HCSB

[28] The following is an excerpt from *The Central Thought of God*, by Witness Lee:

https://www.ministrysamples.org/excerpts/CHRIST-ON-THE-CROSS-DEALING-WITH-SIX-ITEMS-RELATED-TO-SATAN.HTML

"Therefore, we see that with Satan sin came in, death came in, sinners were constituted, and a world was formed, organized, and systematized. In addition, there is the kingdom of darkness, that is, the kingdom of Satan with the rulers, the authorities, the world-rulers of this darkness, the spiritual forces of evil in the heavenlies (Eph. 6:12). All these things are related to Satan. This is a satanic group consisting of six items: Satan, sin, death, sinners, the systematized world, and the kingdom of darkness. On the negative side, these are the matters that the Scriptures are concerned with. By the cross the Lord put the enemy, Satan, to death (Heb. 2:14).

He also died as the One who was made sin for us (2 Cor. 5:21), and He died for our sins (1 Cor. 15:3). All sins are the fruits of sin. Thus, on the cross He solved the problem of sin with its sins. Not only so, the Lord tasted death on the cross (Heb. 2:9) and thus solved the problem of death. Furthermore, on the cross the Lord has crucified the sinful man. Galatians 2:20a says that we have been crucified with Him, and Romans 6:6 says that our old man has been crucified with

Christ. Then, what about the world? The world has also been judged by the Lord on the cross (John 12:31; Gal. 6:14b). When man was put to death on the cross, Satan, who was within man, was also put to death, and the world which belongs to Satan was judged on the cross. Moreover, according to Colossians 2:15, the kingdom of darkness with the rulers and authorities was stripped off by Christ on the cross. Thus, it is only by the cross that the Lord has dealt with and is still dealing with this satanic group of items."

[29] Exodus 36:26, NIV

[30] John 3:3, NIV

[31] 2 Corinthians 5:17, ESV

[32] Ecclesiastes 7:20, NLT

[33] 2 Peter 2:22 NIV

[34] Romans 7:14-25 (VOICE)

[35] Galatians 2:9, 11-14, NIV

[36] James 1:5, ESV

[37] Needham, David. *Birthright: Christian, Do You Know Who You Are?* Sisters, OR: Multnomah Books, 2005.

[38] Isaiah 7:14, NIV written between 701-681 BC

[39] Genesis 22:14, NIV

[40] 1 Chronicles 4:11, NIV

[41] Joshua 5:9, NIV

[42] Genesis 26:18, 20-22, NIV

[43] Genesis 33:20, NIV

[44] 1 King 7:21, 2 Samuel 18:18, NIV

[45] Matthew 27:8, NIV

[46] Esau: hairy. Careah: bald.

[47] Deborah: bee. Jonah: dove. Rachel: ewe. Tamar: palm tree. Susanna: lily.

[48] Holman Bible Dictionary on Naming
 https://www.studylight.org/dictionaries/hbd/n/naming.html

[49] Genesis 17:6, NIV

[50] Genesis 32:22-28, NIV

[51] Matthew 16:13-20, John 1:42, NIV

[52] Daniel 1:3-7, NIV

[53] Ruth 1:19-20, NIV

[54] Luke 1:57-66, NIV, Why John Was Not Named "Little Zach" (Luke 1:57-80) by Robert L. (Bob) Deffinbaugh, Th.M. and pastor/teacher and elder at Community Bible Chapel in Richardson, Texas
https://bible.org/seriespage/why-john-was-not-named-little-zach-luke-157-80

[55] Matthew 5:3-12, NIV

[56] From a sign

[57]https://www.warpaths2peacepipes.com/native-american-indian-names/

[58] Revelation 3:1, NASB

[59] Acts 17:11 NIV

[60] Judges 6-8, ESV

[61] Exodus 19 and Deuteronomy 26 among many others

[62] Deuteronomy 28 and Isaiah 10 among many others

[63] Jonah 1-4, NIV

[64] 2 Samuel 11-12, NIV

[65] 1 Samuel 13:14, NIV

[66] Acts 7-28, NIV and other books Paul authored in the New Testament

[67] Philippians 4:37, NIV

[68] Acts 22:3, NIV

[69] 1 Corinthians 9:19 NIV

[70] Philippians 1:21 NIV

[71] Philemon 1 VOICE

[72] Ephesians 1:17-19, VOICE

[73] The following is excerpted from the article "Who Really Has the Authority on Earth, God or Satan?" by Tim Augustyn (https://www.crosswalk.com/faith/bible-study/who-really-has-the-authority-on-earth-god-or-satan.html).

What Kind of Authority Does Satan Exercise?

Jesus referred to him as "the ruler of this world" (John 12:31), and Paul calls him "the prince of the power of the air" (Ephesians 2:2) and "the god of this world" (2 Corinthians 4:4). John makes a further distinction when he says: "We know that we are of God, and the whole world is in the power of the evil one" (1 John 5:19). These references leave us with the question: In what sense does Satan "rule" the world?

The Bible frequently uses "the world" or "this world" to refer to the present evil system of opposition to God. So, the Bible never teaches that Satan actually rules over the entire world, but that he is ruler over the current system of sinful opposition to God. In other words, he's leading the rebellion against God.

Satan's Limited Authority

The book of Job gives further insight into the limited nature of Satan's power. Satan came before God with other heavenly beings (Job 1:6), and God asked him where he had been (1:7). Satan tells him, and God asks if he knows about his servant, Job (1:8). Satan challenges God, saying he's put a hedge around him and blessed him, and he asks God to take away the hedge, threatening that if he did, Job would curse God to his face (1:10-11). God removes the hedge of blessing around Job's life, but restricts Satan's activity. It is clear from this that Satan could do only what God had given him permission to do, and nothing more. Job was certainly a believer, but there is no reason to think that Satan somehow has unrestricted

authority over unbelievers. This Scripture tells us the reason that Satan has any authority at all, because God allows it to be so...for now.

All the Kingdoms of the World and Their Authority

Back to your question: If Jesus had bowed his knee to him, could Satan really have given "all the kingdoms of the world and their glory" (Matthew 4:8) to him? If we take what we've learned so far, we can reframe the situation a bit. The kingdoms of the world are made up of people and systems in rebellion against God. Satan was essentially tempting Jesus to join his rebellion against God.

How would Jesus do this? By choosing to bypass God's plan for him to humble himself, die on the cross for our sins, rise to new life, and receive the kingdom of God from his Father (Ephesians 2:5-10). Instead of bowing to God, and being obedient to him, Jesus could bow to Satan, avoid the pain and suffering of the cross, and immediately become king of Satan's rogue kingdom.

Why the Son of God Took on Flesh and Blood

Yes, Satan could have given this kingdom to Jesus. But the very reason that the Son of God took on flesh and blood was "that through death he might render powerless him who had the power of death, that is, the devil" (Hebrews 2:14). When Jesus died on the cross, he took away our sins, satisfying the demands of God's law, and he triumphed over Satan, disarming the power that he holds over people—the power of death, because sin leads to death (Colossians 2:13-15).

Instead of joining his rebellion, Jesus now waits for the final judgment and the decisive victory over Satan to be accomplished, when he will be "thrown into the lake of fire" and "tormented day and night for ever and ever" (Revelation 20:10), and his kingdom and authority will be taken away from Satan and given back to King Jesus, its rightful Author and Owner. Amen."

John 17:14-19, VOICE

Romans 12:2, NIV

1 John 2:15, NIV

[74] Proverbs 18:10, ESV

[75] Jeremiah 33:3, ESV

[76] Matthew 7:15-20. I want to be extremely clear that I love and believe in the calling of a true Christian Evangelist. One of my closest friends travels the world speaking to millions of people proclaiming the Good News of Jesus. What I am referring to here are those who are wolves in sheep's clothing.

[77] Deuteronomy 31:6, NIV

[78] Proverbs 13:13 ESV

[79] Proverbs 18:2 ESV

[80] Proverbs 12:15 ESV

[81] Proverbs 15:1 ESV

[82] Ephesians 4:26 ESV

[83] James 1:19-20 ESV

[84] 1 King 19:11-13, NIV

[85] Psalm 46:10, NIV

[86] Psalm 19, NIV

[87] 1 Samuel 13:14 NIV

[88] Psalm 13, VOICE

[89] Psalm 62:5, ESV

[90] Isaiah 64:8 NIV

[91] Leviticus 22:32, 1 Chronicles 16:10, Psalm 99:3, Luke 1:49, NIV

[92] Titus 1:2, James 1:17, ESV

[93] 1 Peter 2:24, ESV

[94] Joshua 5:13-15, NIV

[95] Matthew 12:30, NLT

[96] Mautz, Scott. "A New Deloitte Study of 10,455 Millennials Shows They Need Help Improving These 4 Skills." Inc.com. Inc., May 21, 2018. https://www.inc.com/scott-mautz/new-deloitte-study-of-10455-millennials-says-employers-are-failing-to-help-young-people-develop-4-crucial-skills.html.

[97] Acts 8:26-40, VOICE

[98] Genesis 50:20 NIV

[99] Matthew 6:8, NIV

[100] 1 John 5:14-15, NIV

[101] Romans 5:8, VOICE

102 John 8:32, NIV

103 Isaiah 43:25 NIV

104 James 4:10, NIV

105 Luke 4:18, VOICE

106 Romans 8:14, NIV

107 I Samuel 15:22-24, Jeremiah 7:21-23, NIV

108 Philippians 4:4-7, VOICE

109 Luke 5:16, NIV

110 Mark 1:35, ESV

111 Luke 22:41, NIV

112 Hebrews 11, NIV

113 Luke 7:1-10, NIV, The faith of the centurion: "I tell you, I have not found such great faith even in Israel."
Mark 6:1-7, NIV, A Prophet without honor: "He was amazed at their lack of faith."

114 John 10:27, NIV

115 1 John 1:9, NIV

116 Jeremiah 29:13, NIV

117 Mark 9:23-25, ESV

J. Michael Valdes grew up in the Pacific Northwest and resides with his beautiful wife, Erin, and their four children (Ranger, Arabella, Andie and Storm) in Tualatin, Oregon.

Since 2001, Jeff has been drawn to work with those indigenous people (most of who are unable to receive any formal education), in relatively unknown villages that lack paved roads, consistent electricity and running water. In response, his *Fearless Teacher* identity led him to start The Berean Way, a ministry to partner with many of the forgotten people of the world in places that include Uganda, India, Sri Lanka, Nepal, Myanmar, Nicaragua among several other countries. He has also been a business consultant for over 30 years.

Jeff only recently discovered his love of writing and this hopes to be the first of several titles. Look for his follow up book, *Free and Unleashed: Loving Family, Friends and Enemies* coming next year.

The Key Logo

Jeff and Calli spent a long time developing and designing this logo for you. Our goal was to create something common and simple, yet profound.

The idea derives from Chapter 3 and is best summarized by the imprint on its side, *SINGLE USE ONLY.*

Three circles represent the source of the key through the trinity of the Father, the Son and the Holy Spirit. The overall skeleton-type key design has been used in actual prisons for generations to release prisoners from their captivity.

Although we were *all* born in a prison of sorts and trapped by our false identities of fear, anxiety, guilt and shame, freedom has been generously provided to everyone.

I hope you embrace the symbolism of this key to unlock your jail cell so you can walk away forever and discover why you should follow Jesus into a new world He has for you.

Only then can you be Alive & Free in your true identity.

Pointillism

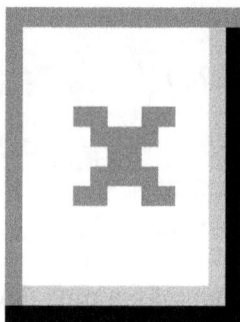

Calli Luikart

Calli Luikart grew up in Portland, Oregon as the middle of three siblings. Her hard work and independent spirit led her to start working full-time since the age of 16. Although art had been her passion since she was young, she chose to pursue more *practical* business degrees which led her to Nashville, TN on the other side of the country. She graduated Belmont University with majors in Accounting and Management.

Just weeks before graduation, Calli was in a life-changing accident that left her paralyzed from the chest down. Her journey is extraordinary and well documented on her Caring Bridge link.

After the accident, Calli's hope for her future seemed all but lost. Reality sunk in and her perception of her identity was going to be much different than what she had envisioned.

Not only was she learning how to live with paralysis, she had little to no function in her hands. Calli's occupational therapist created a brace for her hand, and from there she discovered a new form of art called pointillism.

Now embracing her true identity, several platforms have been opened up for Calli. God has used her to encourage thousands around the world through her stories, public speaking and art. Her journey has only just begun.

You can discover more about Calli's art at her website www.luikartink.com.